The Fiction Writer's Guide *to* Dialogue

The Fiction Writer's Guide *to* Dialogue

A Fresh Look at an Essential Ingredient of the Craft

John Hough, Jr.

ALLWORTH PRESS
NEW YORK

Allworth Press books may be purchased in bulk at special discounts for sales promotion, corporate gifts, fund-raising, or educational purposes. Special editions can also be created to specifications. For details, contact the Special Sales Department, Allworth Press, 307 West 36th Street, 11th Floor, New York, NY 10018 or info@skyhorsepublishing.com.

25 24 23 22 21   7 6 5 4 3

Published by Allworth Press, an imprint of Skyhorse Publishing, Inc.
307 West 36th Street, 11th Floor, New York, NY 10018.
Allworth Press® is a registered trademark of Skyhorse Publishing, Inc.®, a Delaware corporation.

www.allworth.com

Cover design by Mary Belibasakis
Cover photo credit Thinkstock

Library of Congress Cataloging-in-Publication Data is available on file.

Print ISBN: 978-1-62153-439-6
Ebook ISBN: 978-1-62153-449-5

Printed in the United States of America

CONTENTS

INTRODUCTION: Dialogue is Character

A friend of mine, an emeritus professor of American history at one of the country's best liberal arts colleges, decided to write a novel in his retirement. It was a reasonable ambition; he was the author of four books and a lecturer of considerable eloquence and subtlety. He wrote a hundred pages, and an agent read them.

She declined to represent him. His characters, she said, lacked nuance and depth. They weren't *alive*. He considered the criticism, looked again at his novel, and abandoned the idea of writing fiction.

Why?

"I can't write dialogue," he said.

He was giving up too easily, but his appreciation of dialogue as essential to good fiction was on the money. "A man or woman who does not write good dialogue is not a first-rate writer," declared the late George V. Higgins, and while it may not always have been true—the musty dialogue of Henry James comes to mind—I can't think of a first-rate writer today who doesn't write good dialogue. Think of it as one of your most efficient tools, if not *the* most—a component that by itself can elevate your story or novel to literary excellence.

There is no great fiction without great characters, a truth going back to Odysseus and beyond. In the end, it is characters, far more than story, that make fiction great. Characters are the novelist's lifetime gift to the reader. Think of Charles Dickens and you find yourself wandering a portrait gallery of old friends: Mr. Micawber, Lady Dedlock, the Artful Dodger, Ebenezer Scrooge, Betsey Trotwood, and on and on. Who remembers the plot of *Treasure Island* years after reading it, beyond a general idea of the voyage and mutiny? But Long John Silver, one of literature's most winsome villains, is as alive in our memory today as the day we put the book down. To read *Huckleberry Finn* at any age is to acquire a lifelong intimacy with Huck, Jim, Huck's drunken, snake-mean father, and the two cunning rapscallions who call themselves the Duke and the Dauphin. Story does count, of course, but our investment in a story, our capacity to care what happens, runs only as deep as our belief in the humanity of the characters.

Dialogue puts that humanity on vivid display. Characters are never more alive than when they're speaking. To hear them is to see them up close: their physiognomy in fine detail, their expressions, the animation, or lack of it, in their eyes.

"Whosoever of ye," says Captain Ahab, exhorting his crew on the deck of the *Pequod*, "raises me a white-headed whale with a wrinkled brow and a crooked jaw; whosoever of ye raises me that white-headed whale, with three holes punctured in his starboard fluke—look ye, whosoever raises me that same white whale, he shall have this gold ounce, my boys!"

Ahab's obsession, his encroaching madness, ring out in that passionate utterance. We can hear his rising voice, we can *see* him: his avid face, the manic light in his eyes. Could a moment, or a character, be more vivid?

"Action is character," wrote F. Scott Fitzgerald, meaning that characters in fiction define themselves most completely and reliably not by what they think and feel, but by what they *do*. Action is revelatory in a way that thought, opinion, emotion—felt but not expressed—are not. Your character may have an aversion to the killing of animals, which tells us she's humane, moral, evolved. Important, sure, but what happens when she encounters a deer jacker gutting his kill in her woodlot? What does she say, what does she do? Now we find out who she really is.

A half century after Fitzgerald's dead-on pronouncement, George V. Higgins revised Fitzgerald's axiom: "Dialogue is character." Higgins was really clarifying, not rewriting, Fitzgerald's dictum, because dialogue *is* action, as Fitzgerald surely understood. There are telling moments of sudden violent action in *The Great Gatsby*—the death of Myrtle Wilson, Tom Buchanan breaking his mistress's nose—but the novel's two great characters, Jay Gatsby and Daisy Buchanan, with her "low, thrilling voice," reveal and define themselves throughout the novel with their pregnant and idiosyncratic dialogue. Nick Carraway has brought them together after their long separation, and Gatsby has led them from Nick's house to his and is showing them around. Daisy notices a photograph on the bureau:

"I adore it," exclaimed Daisy. "The pompadour! You never told me you had a pompadour—or a yacht."

"Look at this," said Gatsby quickly. "Here's a lot of clippings—about you."

They stood side by side examining it . . . The phone rang, and Gatsby took up the receiver.

"Yes . . . Well, I can't talk now . . . I can't talk now, old sport . . . I said a small town . . . He must know what a small town is . . . Well, he's no use to us if Detroit is his idea of a small town . . ."

He rang off.

"Come here quick!" cried Daisy at the window. The rain was still falling, but the darkness had parted in the west, and there was a pink and golden billow of foamy clouds above the sea.

"Look at that," she whispered, and then after a moment: "I'd like to just get one of those pink clouds and put you in it and push you around."

Dialogue is character: Higgins proved his point brilliantly in his first and best novel, *The Friends of Eddie Coyle*. Nearly eighty percent of this rich and riveting crime novel is dialogue, and every character—bank robbers, a shady saloon keeper, a wily federal agent, and Eddie Coyle himself, family man and petty criminal—is intensely alive. Meet Eddie Coyle, "the stocky man," talking to a young gun dealer, in the opening scene of the novel:

The stocky man extended the fingers of his left hand over the gold-speckled Formica tabletop. "You know what that is?"

"Your hand," Jackie Brown said.

"I hope you look closer at guns 'n you look at that hand," the stocky man said. "Look at your own goddamned hand."

Jackie Brown extended the fingers of his left hand. "Yeah," he said.

"Count your fucking knuckles," the stocky man said.

"All of them?" Jackie Brown said.

"Ah Christ," the stocky man said. "Count as many of them as you want. I got four more. One on each finger. Know how I got those? I bought some stuff from a man that I had his name, and it got traced, and the man I bought it for, he went to M C I Walpole for fifteen to twenty-five. Still in there, but he had some friends. I got an extra set of knuckles. Shut my hand in a drawer. Then one of them stomped the drawer shut."

Eddie is philosophical about what was done to him. He accepts it as logical, even fair. He's no crybaby, and he doesn't hold grudges. Live, learn, and don't make the same mistake twice. It's a glimpse into the mind, if not the heart, of Eddie Coyle.

Characters often reveal themselves in their dialogue without meaning to. The dyed-blonde with the velvet flowers in her hair in Dorothy Parker's acerbic short story, *Arrangement in Black and White*, puts her small mind on display without being prompted, and without knowing it. The reader knows her better than she knows herself. She is talking to her hostess at a cocktail party in honor of the black musician, Walter Williams:

"That's the way I feel," she said. "I just can't understand people being narrow-minded. Why, I absolutely think it's a privilege to meet a man like Walter Williams. Yes, I do. I haven't any feeling at all. Well, my goodness, the good Lord made him, just the same as He did any of us. Didn't He?"

"Surely," said her host. "Yes, indeed."

"That's what I say," she said. "Oh, I get so furious when people are narrow-minded about colored people. It's just all I can do not to say something. Of course, I do admit when you get a bad colored man, they're simply terrible. But as I say to Burton, there are some bad white people, too, in this world. Aren't there?"

"I guess there are," said her host.

"Why, I'd really be glad to have a man like Walter Williams come to my house and sing for us, some time," she said. "Of course, I couldn't ask him on account of Burton, but I wouldn't have any feeling about it at all."

Parker wrote *Arrangement in Black and White* in 1927, a year after the publication of Ernest Hemingway's *The Sun Also Rises* and two years before William Faulkner's *The Sound and the Fury*. All three—Parker, Hemingway, Faulkner—were writing dialogue in a brash new way, bringing to it a new bluntness and economy.

Hemingway was a master of the short story, and his dialogue was never more taut than in his short fiction. From *The Short Happy Life of Francis Macomber*:

"If you make a scene I'll leave you, darling," Margot said quietly.

"No, you won't"

"You can try it and see."

"You won't leave me."

"No," she said, "I won't leave you and you'll behave yourself."

"Behave myself? That's a way to talk. Behave myself."

"Yes. Behave yourself."

"Why don't you try behaving?"

"I've tried it so long. So very long."

Dialogue has always revealed character, but now it was becoming cleaner and more relentlessly direct, as if the speakers were under orders to get straight to the point. The studied attention to dialogue by these three—and, a little later, by John Steinbeck, Katherine Anne Porter, Robert Penn Warren, and others—was transformational. Dialogue had become an art form.

> **"It is worth remembering that Hemingway was writing closer to Dickens's time than to ours."**

It is worth remembering that Hemingway was writing closer to Dickens's time than to ours. His dialogue is often sentimental and can feel mannered, as Faulkner's and Parker's can. The dialogue of all three feels dated at times. But the spare, confrontational dialogue of today's best writers is their legacy. That legacy is their gift to all of us. Take advantage. If you can write good dialogue, you're a writer.

1

THE MECHANICS OF DIALOGUE: TAGS, TALKING VERBS, AND PUNCTUATION

DIALOGUE TAGS AND WHEN TO USE THEM

Dialogue tags are for clarity, obviously—we need to know who is speaking—but when only two people are present, the dialogue is often tagged nevertheless. Why? There are no rules, and so dialogue tags are up to the judgment, instinct, or whim of the writer. They do matter, so consider them as you write. Don't use or omit them automatically.

It takes about a second to read, "she said," but that second checks the flow of the exchange, creating a minute pause. The reader hardly notices, but the pause is there. This can be a consideration when the dialogue is anxious or heated and your two characters are pressing each other. Do you want to touch the brake at all? Maybe not. The young man called Milkman, the protagonist of Toni Morrison's rite-of-passage novel, *Song of Solomon,* is sitting in a barroom booth across from his friend, Guitar. Guitar asks Milkman why he has summoned him here, and Milkman says that he has just knocked his father down:

> "Hit him. Knocked him into the fuckin radiator."
> "What'd he do to you?"
> "Nothin."
> "Nothin? You just upped and popped him?"
> "Yeah."

"For no reason?"

"He hit my mother."

"Oh."

"He hit her. I hit him."

"That's tough."

"Yeah."

"I mean it."

"I know."

Guitar is having trouble believing what Milkman has told him, and his incredulity gives his questions an inquisitorial edge. Milkman is himself surprised by what he's done, but his father had transgressed, and Milkman isn't going to downplay hitting him, or apologize for it. Guitar is pressing and Milkman is pressing back, and Morrison dispenses with dialogue tags, letting the lines leap back and forth across the table, as fast as we can read them.

Now look at this exchange from William Kennedy's *Ironweed,* which won the Pulitzer Prize in 1984. The homeless protagonist, Francis Phelan, is walking down a street in Albany with his zany pal, Rudy:

"There's seven deadly sins," Rudy said.

"Deadly? What do you mean deadly?" Francis said.

"I mean daily," Rudy said. "Every day."

"There's only one sin as far as I'm concerned," Francis said.

"There's prejudice."

"Oh yeah. Prejudice. Yes."

"There's envy."

"Envy. Yeah, yup. That's one."

"There's lust."

"Lust, right. Always liked that one."

"Cowardice."

"Who's a coward?"

"Cowardice."

"I don't know what you mean. That word I don't know."

"Cowardice," Rudy said.

"I don't like the coward word. What're you sayin' about coward?"

"A coward. He'll cower up. You know what a coward is? He'll run."

"No, that word I don't know. Francis is no coward. Listen, you know what I like?"

"What do you like?"

"Honesty," Francis said.

"That's another one," Rudy said.

Kennedy tags the first four speeches, slowing the dialogue, keeping it tentative as the two men feel their way into the conversation. Then, as they warm to the subject, dialogue tags all but disappear. There isn't quite the intensity of emotion here that sharpens the exchange between Guitar and Milkman in the bar—this is a philosophical discussion—but it isn't light or casual, either, and the absence of dialogue tags sustains both the prickliness on Francis's side and Rudy's haste to explain what he means and mollify him. The final two lines are tagged: Kennedy touches the brakes as the conversation winds down, concluding on a genial note.

Morrison and Kennedy probably wrote these passages with much less conscious attention to dialogue tags than my parsing suggests. They probably knew, without having to think about it, where they wanted them. No dialogue tags are right or wrong; they're up to the writer, a matter of fine-tuning. Your ear and mine may be different.

I often advise students to read their dialogue aloud to themselves. There's no better way to assess your dialogue tags than to hear them. Are they buttressing the dialogue, or tripping it up? The morning after the Grangerford family takes him in, Huckleberry Finn wakes up and realizes he's forgotten what he told them his name is:

So I laid there about an hour trying to think, and when Buck waked up I says:

"Can you spell, Buck?"

"Yes," he says.

"I bet you can't spell my name," says I.

"I bet you what you dare I can," says he.

"All right," says I, "go ahead."

"G-e-o-r-g-e J-a-x-o-n—there now," he says.

"Well," says I, "you done it, but I didn't think you could."

Days, but not many pages later, Huck sees Buck shoot at Harney Shepherdson from behind a bush, and wants to know why. Same characters, same voices, but the tempo now is very different:

"Did you want to kill him, Buck?"

"Well, I bet I did."

"What did he do to you?"

"Him? He never done nothing to me."

"Well, then, what did you want to kill him for?"

"Why, nothing—only it's on account of the feud."

"What's a feud?"

"Why, where was you raised? Don't you know what a feud is?"

"Never heard of it before—tell me about it."

Every line of speech is tagged in the first scene. The scene is comic, and it unfolds in an almost leisurely way. Twain keeps the brakes on the dialogue, giving us time to enjoy it. There are no dialogue tags in the second colloquy: Buck's blood is up, and Huck wants answers. Sometimes dialogue tags are of minor importance— the dialogue would work almost equally well with or without them—and sometimes they make all the difference.

THE WISDOM OF ELMORE LEONARD AND THE TALKING VERBS

The third of Elmore Leonard's "Ten Rules of Writing," which were published in a primer-sized leather-bound booklet and are available online, is a blanket prohibition: "Never use a verb other than 'said' to carry dialogue."

I run into some resistance to this commandment when I'm teaching, and there are some great modern writers—Eudora Welty, notably—who decline to subscribe to it. (Leonard's dialogue, it should be noted, matches up with anybody's.)

"The line of dialogue belongs to the character," Leonard explains. "The verb is the writer sticking his nose in. But 'said' is far less intrusive than grumbled, gasped, cautioned, lied."

I'd go further: "said" isn't intrusive, at all. It's invisible. The reader reads it again and again and again, and never notices it. The dialogue, then, stands on its own. This forces you, the writer, to write dialogue that needs no help, and dialogue that needs no help is good dialogue.

I don't know what Leonard would have said about "asked" and "answered." Most writers use them, but an answer is obviously an answer, so why not stick with "said"? I'm not a stickler about "asked"—I may have used it myself a few times—but the question mark at the end of the line makes the verb redundant.

I *do* know what Leonard would have said about "continued" and "interrupted"—he never use them. "Continued" is a lumbering verb that treats the reader like . . . well, isn't it obvious that the speaker is continuing? Likewise, an interruption is an interruption and doesn't need to be identified as one. Beginners love the verb for some reason, and again and again I find myself pointing out that the line they've written isn't even an interruption—the previous line is a complete sentence.

From *Ironweed*:

> "If I come back tomorrow . . ."
>
> "We'll see about tomorrow," said the preacher, who grabbed the doorknob himself and pulled it to as he ushered Little Red out into the night.

The preacher stops Little Red in mid-sentence, speaking over him and hurrying him out the door. Who needs to be told that the preacher "interrupted" Little Red?

AVOIDING ADVERBS TO MODIFY "SAID"

Leonard's fourth rule says almost the same thing as his third: "Never use an adverb to modify the verb 'said.'" Adverbs—gravely, angrily, coolly, excitedly—are intrusive, like verbs other than "said." They distract the reader, calling attention away from the dialogue itself. And, like those verbs, they give a line of dialogue help it shouldn't need. Instead of "said gravely," write a grave line of dialogue—a line with gravity we can hear in the words you choose, and in the rhythm and movement of the sentence. Write a slow sentence, a somber one. Write an angry line (this is easy). Write a cool line, an excited one.

I wouldn't tell you never to use "loudly" or "quietly" with "said," but before you do, consider whether it might be possible to write a line that conveys the raised or lowered voice.

A final word. Fitzgerald often modified "said," and even Hemingway did, occasionally, but we chalk that up to their era and pass over it with a forgiving eye. Today, an adverb with "said" has a distinctly old-fashioned flavor. It fits, is at home, in a novel written back in the Jazz Age.

ITALICS IN DIALOGUE

Italicized words are emphatic, sometimes loud, sometimes shrill, and permissible in limited amounts. The best dialogue writers need them only occasionally. Higgins never italicizes dialogue in *The Friends of Eddie Coyle*. He never has to. Here, Jackie Brown, the gun dealer, finds himself under arrest:

> "Do you understand your rights?" Moran said.
> "Yes," Jackie Brown said. "Yes, yes, yes."
> "Shut up," Moran said. "Turn around and hold out your wrists."
> Foley snapped the handcuffs on Jackie Brown's wrists. "You're under

arrest for violation of U. S. Code twenty-six, Section fifty-eight-sixty-one, possession of a machine gun without being registered as the owner and possessor of a machine gun."

"Hey," Jackie Brown said.

"Shut up," Foley said. "I don't want to hear one more fucking word out of you. You keep your goddamned trap shut. Now get in your car."

Read this aloud, and you can't help raising your voice. Expletives usually raise the volume level; it's hard to read them quietly. Moran's voice is under control when he recites the charge against Jackie Brown—the length of the line, as well as the dry legal syntax, bring the level down—but the short lines are snappish. There's voltage in them. They're *loud*. The verb, you'll notice, is always "said," and it is never modified.

EXCLAMATION POINTS

And something else in the dialogue above: in all that heated back-and-forth, there isn't an exclamation point to be seen. Exclamation points are the target of Leonard's fifth rule: "Keep your exclamation points under control. You are allowed no more than two or three per 100,000 words of prose." William Maxwell, novelist and longtime editor of the *New Yorker*, went quite a bit further, asserting that a novelist should be permitted one exclamation point in his or her *career*. Fitzgerald didn't like exclamation points, though he was probably thinking more of exposition than dialogue when he advised a writer friend, "Cut out all those exclamation points. An exclamation point is like laughing at your own joke."

I don't think anything absolute can be said about exclamation points. Even Leonard adds a qualifier to his stricture on them: "If you have the knack of playing with exclaimers the way Tom Wolfe does, you can throw them in by the handful." Wolfe certainly does. From *A Man in Full*:

"This is so funny, because I was thinking about you just yesterday and wondering how to get in touch with you!"

"With me?"

"Yes! There's something I need to run by you. Could I give you
a ring?"

"Well—of course, Mr . . ."

"Peepgass!" he said. "Ray! Make it Ray!"

He produced a ballpoint pen from an inside jacket pocket and
then began ransacking his tuxedo for a piece of paper. Finding none,
he thrust out the cuff of the left sleeve of his shirt and positioned
the pen above it and grinned and said, "What's the number?"

"Not on your shirt! It'll never come out."

"You're right! Here—I'll put it here!" He positioned the pen
over the back of his left hand and grinned some more.

Tom Wolfe earns his exemption from Leonard's fifth rule
because . . . well, because he's Tom Wolfe. Wolfe's narrative voice, as
well his dialogue, are so original and witty, and have been so influ-
ential, that Leonard steps back respectfully and allows Wolfe to go
his own way. The man and woman in the colloquy above, Martha
Croker and Ray Peepgass, are wooing each other awkwardly, both
beset by nervousness. Wolfe slaps on the exclamation points, giving the dialogue a high-pitched, over-eager feel on both sides. If
Elmore Leonard won't fault Wolfe, I certainly won't, but try this:

"Not on your *shirt*. It'll never come out."

"You're right. Here—I'll put it here."

Martha's voice jumps an octave with the italicized *shirt*, and
Peepgass's line comes tumbling out of him, rapid and jumpy, even
without the exclamation point. It's good dialogue, either way. Is it
better without the exclamation points, or has it lost something? I'll
leave that to you.

Eudora Welty's and Anne Tyler's characters, like Wolfe's, are
exclaimers. Lee Smith uses exclamation points somewhat less

frequently. Welty's house in Jackson, Mississippi, is a National Historic Landmark, open to the public as a museum. Tyler's fiction has won a bouquet of awards, including the Pulitzer Prize. And Smith, for my money, is the best American writer not yet to have won either the Pulitzer or the National Book Award. So, if you decide to part company with Elmore Leonard and William Maxwell when it comes to exclamation points, you'll be in good company.

At most, use them sparingly. Don't rely on them, automatically, to characterize a line of dialogue; try first to write an excited line, a nervous one, a loud one. There is also the option of breaking Elmore Leonard's third rule—as Leonard does himself every once in a while—and ratcheting the verb up to a shout, a yell, a holler, a cry. These verbs make an exclamation point unnecessary, but they also accommodate it, when it is there. At the climax of my novel, *Seen the Glory*, Pickett's Charge at Gettysburg, the boy Thomas Chandler, fighting for the Union, follows his brother, Luke, and his best friend, Elisha Smith, toward the pandemonium around the copse:

> "Luke!" Thomas shouted. "Elisha!"
> He could not hear himself. A shell went off in the air ahead of him and another on the ground, percussion, chucking a couple of men in the air, head over heels . . .
> "Elisha! Luke!"

The noise I was trying to describe, gunfire and cannons and exploding shells, was beyond deafening—a percussive thunder that is like nothing Thomas has ever heard. He continues running toward the trees:

> He could not see McNamara or Rivers or Merriman, just the two flags moving deeper into the sulfurous smoke, the gunfire, the exploding shells.
> "Luke!"

I didn't see any way around these exclamation points. I found it a challenge to evoke the noise at that moment—"There's no way to describe it," the chief historian at Gettysburg had told me—and I thought the exclamation points helped to summon up not just the desperation in Thomas's voice, but the din he's yelling into. They were the only exclamation points in the novel. I think there's a happy medium somewhere between William Maxwell's edict and Tom Wolfe's exclaimers, one that we should all look for as we write.

QUOTATION MARKS: THEY'RE OPTIONAL

The dialogue in Kent Haruf's first two novels, *The Tie That Binds* and *Where You Once Belonged,* is enclosed, as most dialogue is, in quotation marks. Then, with *Plainsong,* a finalist for the National Book Award, quotation marks disappeared. Haruf hasn't used them in his three novels since.

There's no rule that says you have to use quotation marks around your dialogue, but their absence is noticed. The reader takes note, adjusts, and reads on. It's the smallest of impositions, but it *is* an imposition, and the writer must have his or her good reasons for asking it. He needs, as well, a certain amount of self-confidence: *I'm doing it my way, and you'll have to live with it. The Tie That Binds* is a wonderful novel, but one can speculate that it wasn't until his success with *Plainsong* that Haruf decided he could disregard the etiquette of quotation marks.

Cormac McCarthy disregarded it from the outset. There are no quotation marks in his first novel, *The Orchard Keeper,* or in any others. Raymond Carver uses quotation marks in most of his short stories, but not all. Charles Frazier, whose first novel, *Cold Mountain,* won the National Book Award in 1997 and was a literary sensation, invented his own alternative to quotation marks, a dash in front of every speech.

The omission of quotation marks is a visual matter, obviously. When read aloud, dialogue without quotation marks sounds no different than it would with them. McCarthy's and Haruf's dialogue is lyrical and clean, and their idea may be that quotation marks would clutter it, as perhaps they would. Frazier's dashes give his dialogue little visual jolts without seeming to touch or compromise it.

Feel free to experiment. Three novels ago, I stopped using quotation marks in flashbacks. My idea was to set the dialogue of the past apart, visually, from that of the present. Flashbacks are memory, and it seemed to me that the absence of quotation marks would give that dialogue a less immediate, more settled, more final feel. Take the chance yourself if it seems right to you, but remember that you're well outside the mainstream when you do.

2

HOW ART DOES NOT IMITATE LIFE

THE WATERGATE TAPES—WHY REAL CONVERSATION MAKES FOR POOR READING

In 1971 President Richard M. Nixon installed voice-activated tape recorders in the suite of rooms in the White House where he conducted business. This putative windfall for future historians was a windfall indeed, but not in the way Nixon intended. The tapes were still rolling a year later, when partisans of the president tried to burglarize the headquarters of the Democratic National Committee in the building called the Watergate, giving the ensuing scandal its name.

The burglars were caught inside the DNC offices and arrested, and before long Watergate was a household word. Nixon and his aides denied everything and, recording themselves, entered into a conspiracy to suppress all inquiry into the matter. A year after the break-in, the Senate Watergate Committee held hearings to get to the bottom of it.

It was during these hearings that a low-level White House employee inadvertently revealed the existence of the tapes—the moment that doomed the Nixon presidency. You can read the transcripts on line today: the president and his aides discussing hush money, subornation of perjury, money laundering, and the playing of dirty tricks on their political opponents.

On June 23, 1972, Nixon and his chief of staff, H. R. Haldeman, discussed the burgeoning FBI investigation of the burglary attempt, which had occurred six days earlier. The recording of this conversation was called the "Smoking Gun Tape." Here is Nixon, talking his way to impeachment, and Haldeman, talking *his* way to imprisonment for obstruction of justice, greatly redacted for brevity:

> Haldeman: Now, on the investigation, you know, the Democratic break-in thing, we're back to the—in the, the problem area because the FBI is not under control . . . and they have, their investigation is now leading into some productive areas, because they've been able to trace the money, not through the money itself, but through the bank, you know, sources . . . And, and it goes in some directions we don't want it to go.
>
> Nixon: Right.
>
> Haldeman: . . . the way to handle this now is for us to have Walters call Pat Gray in and just say, "Stay the hell out of this . . . this is ah, business here we don't want you to go any further on it."
>
> Nixon: Uh huh.
>
> Haldeman: . . . and, uh, that would take care of it.
>
> Nixon: What about Pat Gray, ah, you mean he doesn't want to?
>
> Haldeman: Pat does want to. He doesn't know how to, and he doesn't have, he doesn't have any basis for doing it. Given this, he will then have the basis. He'll call Mark Felt in . . . Ah, he'll call him in and say, "We've got the signal from across the river to, to put the hold on this."
>
> Nixon: Well, I mean, ah, there's no way . . . I'm just thinking if they don't cooperate, what do they say? They, they, they were approached by the Cubans. That's what Dahlberg has to say, the Texans too. Is that the idea?
>
> Haldeman: Well, if they will. But then we're relying on more and more people all the time. That's the problem. And ah, they'll stop if we could, if we take this other step.

Nixon: All right. Fine.

Haldeman: They say the only way to do that is from White House instructions. And it's got to be to Helms and, ah . . . the proposal would be that Ehrlichman and I call them in and say, ah . . .

Nixon: Of course, this is a, this is a hunt, you will—that will uncover a lot of things . . . This involves these Cubans, Hunt, and a lot of hanky-panky that we have nothing to do with ourselves. Well what the hell, did Mitchell know about this thing to any much of a degree?

Haldeman: I don't think he knew the details, but I think he knew.

Nixon: He didn't know how it was going to be handled though. Well who was the asshole that did? Is it Liddy? Is that the fellow? He must be a little nuts.

Haldeman: He is.

Nixon: I mean he just isn't well screwed on is he? Isn't that the problem?

Haldeman: No, but he was under pressure, apparently, to get more information, and as he got more pressure, he pushed the people harder to move harder on . . .

Nixon: Pressure from Mitchell?

Haldeman: Apparently.

Nixon: Oh, Mitchell, Mitchell was at the point that you made on this, that exactly what I need from you is on the–

Haldeman: Gemstone, yeah.

Nixon: All right, fine, I understand it all.

Haldeman: Colson, yesterday, they concluded it was not the White House, but are now convinced it is a CIA thing, so the CIA turn off would . . .

Nixon: When you get in these people when you . . . get these people in, say: "Look, the problem is that this will open the whole, the whole Bay of Pigs thing, and the President just feels that" ah, without going into the details . . . don't, don't lie to them to the extent to say there is no involvement, but just say this is sort of a comedy of errors, bizarre, without getting into it, "the President believes that it is going to open the whole Bay of Pigs thing up again. And, ah, because these people are plugging for, for keeps and that they should call the FBI in and say that we wish for the country, don't go any further into this case," period!

If you skipped any of this—or most of it—I don't blame you. Riveting reading, it is not. It's meandering. It's repetitive. There are pointless-seeming interruptions. Some of it is hard to follow, some of it is nearly unintelligible. What's going on here? Richard Nixon, whatever you think of him, was educated and far from stupid. He was articulate in public. H. R. Haldeman was an advertising executive and a graduate of UCLA. So why is the dialogue between two powerful and intelligent men conniving in a felony so insipid in print?

The answer is all around you, in the dialogue you hear every hour of every day, and in the words you speak yourself. It's the way we talk: the unfinished sentence, the sudden shift of topic, the empty pause, the repetition, the interruptions. In real life we digress. We ramble. We elaborate needlessly. We use three or four sentences, three or four words, where one would do. The three years of the Nixon tapes run to thousands and thousands of pages, and no wonder.

> **The dialogue writer is not a stenographer, writing down what he hears**

As the Watergate tapes demonstrate, dialogue in fiction is *not* derived from real life. If it were, you'd bore the reader, probably confuse him, and triple the length of your novel. The dialogue writer is not a stenographer, writing down what he hears; he's an extrapolator, a rewrite man, bringing coherence to our oral discourse, condensing what we say and giving it shape and cohesion.

KEEPING IT SHORT AND SWEET

Economy is a cardinal rule. As a young newspaper reporter I learned that, whatever you're writing, if you can cut words without losing meaning, you strengthen what remains. Less is more. Don't crowd good words with unnecessary ones; the good words are diminished by the noise around them.

> **If you can cut words without losing meaning, you strengthen what remains.**

This is especially true of dialogue. Not just every sentence or phrase, but every *word* should be indispensable to the meaning or the effect you're aiming for. If you can cut it, you don't need it; it is hurting, not helping. Train your eye to spot the words that sit there without pulling their weight. There might be very little left when you're done, and the dialogue is likely to be excellent. This is from *Song of Solomon*:

> "You want this for the baby's name?"
>
> "I want that for the baby's name. Say it."
>
> "You can't name the baby this."
>
> "Say it."
>
> "It's a man's name."
>
> "Say it."
>
> "Pilate."
>
> "What?"
>
> "Pilate. You wrote down Pilate."
>
> "Like a river boat pilot?"
>
> "No. Not like no riverboat pilot. Like a Christ-killing Pilate. You can't get much worse than that for a name. And a baby girl at that."

The artistry here is in the brevity, the compactness of the lines. Every speech but the last one is comprised of a single sentence. Some are two and even one word long. We don't talk like this in real life. We don't speak with such precision and clarity and directness.

You can't always get away with giving a character a speech of one sentence, but do it when you can. And unless a character is musing out

Make this a rule—one to three sentences, preferably no more than two, per speech— whenever possible.

loud, delivering a rant, or telling a story, aim for speeches of no more than three sentences. Make this a rule—one to three sentences, preferably no more than two, per speech—whenever possible.

The rule will help you discipline yourself. Follow it, and you won't allow your characters to digress. You won't allow them to repeat themselves. They won't be likely to drop a subject and move to another in mid-speech, which can throw dialogue into confusion. The rule will also save you from what I've found to be the most common of writing students' mistakes: the sentence that repeats an idea, emotion, or fact, expressing it in different words.

We do this almost automatically in real life. In the Watergate tapes Haldeman says he's going to instruct Patrick Gray to "stay the hell out of this." He will tell Gray: "This is ah, business here, we don't want you to go any further on it." Same thought—Gray has to be muzzled—expressed in a different way.

Nixon asks a question. "Well, who was the asshole that did? Is it Liddy? Is that the fellow?" Same question, three times, and note how its impact is diminished with each reiteration.

Short speeches keep the dialogue, and the narrative, moving at a brisk pace, which never hurts, and which is especially important in tense situations. The transcript of a real confrontation between a high school teacher and problem student would be more verbose and wandering than this exchange between the teacher Guthrie and his least favorite student in Haruf's *Plainsong*:

> That's it? Guthrie said. You think that just about covers it?
> Yeah.
> That was pretty short.
> I couldn't find anything, the boy said.
> You couldn't find anything about Thomas Jefferson?

No.

The Declaration of Independence.

No.

The presidency. His life at Monticello.

No.

Where did you look?

Everywhere I could think of.

You must not have thought very long," Guthrie said. Let me see your notes.

I just got this page.

Let me see that much.

The boy's answers come across as sullen and disrespectful *because* they're so brief. He isn't bothering to explain himself, and Guthrie isn't bothering to cajole the boy or offer him a chance to reconsider. Haruf boils the quarrel down to its essence—to short tight sentences that impel the exchange quickly along. You don't hear dialogue like it in real life. You have to make it up.

WHEN SHORT AND SWEET ISN'T ENOUGH

Of course you need a fourth sentence sometimes, or a fifth, a sixth, and more. But by the sixth sentence, if not sooner, your character has begun to run on, and the interaction, for the moment, is suspended. The other character, or characters, have become listeners, and the drama shifts to the text of the speech itself. Drama requires tension, which I'll get to in the next chapter; the point here is that economy is as important in long speeches as in short ones. Don't let your characters ramble, or repeat themselves without reason.

The baby is sick, and Hank Smith and Katie Cocker, the country singer, are arguing in Lee Smith's novel about a musical family from the Virginia hills, *The Devil's Dream*. Katie is narrating:

"I'm going to take her to the hospital if I have to walk," I said.

"You are not! You spoil that baby to death, Katie, that's probably what's the matter with her anyway. It's nothing, I'm telling you. Get in bed. I've got to get up at six o'clock and go to work, in case you've forgotten."

Hank shouts Katie down—what can she do but listen? He snatches her attention, and ours, and holds it with dialogue that is swollen with petulance and denial and plain laziness. The chips are down and Hank is revealing who he really is; Katie is learning something, and so are we, and it's more than enough to keep us reading. All this—count them—in five sentences.

William Kennedy's admirable street bum, Francis Phelan, tells a couple of friends what he'd do if he had fifty dollars:

"I had fifty, I'd spend it on her," Francis said. "Or buy a pair of shoes. Other pair wore out and Harry over at the old clothes joint give 'em to me for a quarter. He seen me half barefoot and says, Francis you can't go around like that, and he give me these. But they don't fit right and I only got one of 'em laced. Twine there in the other one. I got a shoestring in my pocket but ain't put it in yet."

This quiet speech is about as perfect as dialogue gets. There's a little story in it of poverty and kindness. Each line is meticulously crafted in the spare vernacular of the hobo. Seven sentences.

In *Song of Solomon* the Reverend Cooper tells Milkman how he came by the permanent lump behind his ear:

"Some of us went to Philly to try and march in an Armistice Day parade. This was after the First World War. We were invited and had a permit, but the people, the white people, didn't like us being there. They started a fracas. You know, throwing rocks and calling us names. They didn't care nothing 'bout the uniform.

Anyway, some police on horseback came—to quiet them down, we thought. They ran us down. Right under their horses. This here's what a hoof can do. Ain't that something?"

There's a story here, containing racial bigotry, violence, and some American history, told in eight sentences. Three of these sentences are very short. There are longer speeches in *Song of Solomon*—some fill more than a page—but the speakers never repeat themselves, they never veer off the subject. Ten sentences, twenty: they should be as lean and substantive as the Reverend Cooper's eight.

There's no easy way to write dialogue like this. Superfluous words and phrases come naturally to us when we talk and when we write. Observe the one-to-three sentence rule as consistently as you can. Dole out that fourth sentence—and the fifth, and the sixth—grudgingly. Pretend that every line of dialogue is costly. Don't buy it unless you have to.

KEEPING IT UNREAL: AVOIDING THE QUIRKS, TICS, AND HABITS OF REAL LIFE

We develop certain habits when we talk to each other, usually by common consensus; take a pledge against most of them when you write dialogue.

Don't begin a question with "So," as in, "So, Sharon, how do you like being the mother of triplets?" Or, "So, Eddie, did you win the game last night?" In real life we do this almost instinctively, as a matter of consideration or courtesy. That prefatory *So*, usually followed by the addressee's name, makes the question less abrupt. It softens it, begins it on a tentative note, as if to say, *If you don't mind my asking . . .*

This is the last thing you want in your dialogue. Dialogue *should* be abrupt. Every question, however benign, should be direct. It should demand an answer. With every question, your characters are putting each other on the spot, which is why their answers are revealing.

Katie Cocker and Ralph Handy are sitting in a diner and falling in love in *The Devil's Dream:*

> "What are you grinning at?" Ralph asked me.
> "You," I said real bold. "I'm grinning at you."

It's the abruptness of Ralph's question that makes it good. It catches Katie by surprise and she answers "real bold," matching boldness with boldness. *So, Katie, what are you grinning at?*—write it this way, and you transform the question. You make it more casual, less probing. You put a note of hesitation in it. You make it easier to answer.

Keep your characters from stating the obvious.

Keep your characters from stating the obvious. Here is one of the major differences between dialogue in fiction and in real life. In real life we say, "That's beautiful." Or, "That's funny." Or, "That's awful." Or, "That's sad." Unless these observations somehow contradict the evidence, we're stating what is obvious. "I'm so relieved," you say, when it turns out you don't need a hip replacement. Of course you're relieved—it goes without saying. "This complicates things," you say, when your lawyer tells you there's a labyrinthine codicil to your father's will. No kidding.

When it comes to dialogue in fiction, this natural impulse to say the obvious about the situation at hand is dead weight. There's no need for your characters to tell each other, and the reader, that bad news is bad news, or that beauty is beauty. "I'm glad to see you" is a bad line when two old friends meet. So is "I'm sorry for your loss" when a friend's father has passed. Of course they're glad, of course they're sorry.

An expletive as an interjection, spoken in anger or disappointment, is usually a bad line; the four-letter word when your character finds himself locked out of his house is an obvious response. (See more on expletives in chapter seven.) If your character is pounding on a door, never have her say "Let me in!" or "Open up!"—the pounding says it, the demand states what is already clear.

In beginners' fiction I often come across the line, "I can't believe this is happening." Avoid this line like the plague. You hear it regularly in real life, and you probably say it yourself from time to time, in a wide range of circumstances. You're at the airport, soon to board your flight to France, and you discover you've left your passport at home. *I can't believe this is happening.* Your car breaks down on the highway at one in the morning. *I can't believe this is happening.* You're indicted for a crime you didn't commit. *I can't believe this is happening.* But it *is* happening, and it is so far from what you expected that you can't help saying so, stating what is painfully obvious. *Never* use this line in your dialogue.

In real life we talk around things, we speak idly, but all dialogue in fiction has to reveal something. It has to contain news of some sort, and there's no news in a statement of the obvious unless the statement itself is the news. The kindly elderly priest learns that someone has stolen Sunday's collection money and states the obvious, "This is bad!" embroidering it with obscenities. There's news in the line if we haven't yet heard the priest cuss. If your characters are going to state the obvious, they must do it in a surprising way.

The sheriff's deputy, Wendell, states the obvious in Cormac McCarthy's *No Country For Old Men,* when he and Sheriff Bell come upon a crime scene in the desert, a strew of bodies, bullet-riddled cars and pickups, a dog shot and killed:

> It's a mess, ain't it, Sheriff?
> If it ain't, it'll have to do till one gets here.

A mess: the laconic understatement makes Wendell's line interesting. It isn't a word we expect. Sheriff Bell's laconic answer does him one better, so wry and whimsical it makes the reader smile.

OMITTING GREETINGS AND SALUTATIONS

Omit the pleasantries, greetings, and salutations that open conversations in real life. Go straight to the dialogue that matters. Maggie Jones, the schoolteacher in *Plainsong*, drives out to the elderly McPheron brothers' farm:

> They got down and approached her slowly, calmly, as deliberately as church deacons, as if they were not at all surprised to see her. They moved heavily in their winter coveralls and they had on thick caps pulled low and cumbersome winter gloves.
>
> You're going to freeze yourself, standing there, Harold said. You better get out of this wind. Are you lost?
>
> Probably, Maggie Jones said. She laughed. But I wanted to talk to you.

Encounters in real life sometimes do begin as summarily as this; in fiction they must, always. Standard greetings and courtesies don't reveal character or move the story, they only delay things. The reader might assume that your characters have already said hello to each other, or he might not. You're fine, either way; the reader isn't going to spend a moment wondering about it.

PHONE CONVERSATIONS

Strip telephone conversations down to what matters. Never, without a good reason, use "hello" or "good-bye."

From *The Friends of Eddie Coyle:*

> In the telephone booth, Eddie deposited a dime and dialed a Boston number. He said: "Foley there?"

Someone speaks to Eddie first on the other end, but we don't hear it. We don't need to; if we did, Higgins would have written it.

The actress Maria Wyeth, the protagonist of Joan Didion's short novel of excess and loneliness in Hollywood, *Play It As It Lays*, is on the phone with her friend Felicia Goodwin:

> "Les finished the script?"
>
> "I'll get him," Felicia said with relief.
>
> "Never mind," Maria said, but it was too late.
>
> "Where've you been," he said.
>
> "Nowhere." When she heard his voice she felt a rush of well-being. "I didn't want to call because—"
>
> "I can't hear you, Maria, where are you?"
>
> "In a phone booth. I just wanted—"
>
> "You all right?"
>
> "No. I mean yes." A bus was shifting gears on Sunset and she raised her voice. "Listen. Call me."
>
> She walked back to the car and sat for a long while . . .

Do Les Goodwin and Maria say hello to each other when he comes on the phone? Do they say good-bye after Les ends the conversation with "Call me"? The question doesn't occur to us.

WHEN AND HOW TO USE REPETITION

Don't let your characters repeat what was just said in the form of a question, as a prelude to their response, as we often do in real life. I see this in beginners' fiction almost as often as I hear it in daily conversation. It goes like this:

"What time is it, Joe?"

"What time is it? It's nine o'clock."

Or:

"I saw a giraffe yesterday."

"A giraffe? Where?"

It's the question mark that usually makes this repetition fatal. I say *usually*; a character might repeat what he's just heard in a reaction of bafflement or incredulity. Short of that, the repetition is rhetorical and meaningless.

I made this point in a workshop one time, and later, on another subject, read this exchange aloud from McCarthy's *All the Pretty Horses,* the first volume of his Border Trilogy:

> What did you do?
> I walked up behind him and snatched it out of his belt. That's what I done.
> And shot him.
> He come at me.
> Come at you.
> Yeah.
> So you shot him.
> What choice did I have?
> What choice, said John Grady.
> I didn't want to shoot the dumb son of a bitch. That was never no part of my intention.

After I'd read this, a student jumped all over me. *Come at you. What choice*—John Grady Cole is repeating what Jimmy Blevins just said.

"Look at it again," I said. "These aren't questions. John Grady heard him loud and clear."

John Grady—he is John Grady Cole, the protagonist of *All the Pretty Horses* and *Cities of the Plain*—repeats what the boy Jimmy Blevins has said, affirming it both times in a spirit of both incredulity and challenge. *He come at me*: John Grady can scarcely believe what he's heard, and he throws Blevins's answer back at him as if for further consideration. As if to say, *Listen to yourself.* Blevins's question, *What choice did I have?* is rhetorical, and it is also preposterous. *What choice.* John Grady repeats it in amazement, again turning the question back on Blevins, who had plenty of choices besides killing the man.

Try it this way:

> He come at me.
> Come at you?

And again:

> He come at me.
> Come at you.

The repeated line, without a question mark, is tendentious. With the question mark, it sounds mildly, and oddly, puzzled. It turns the line slack.

Repetition can be useful to drive a point home, or to hold on to it, keep it in play. In McCarthy's *The Crossing*, the second volume of the Border Trilogy, Billy Parham, a civilian, goes into a Texas bar during World War II and receives a chilly reception from the barman and a soldier:

> Do you know how old I am? the barman said.
> Billy looked at him. No, he said. How would I know how old you are?
> I'll be thirty-eight years old in June. June fourteenth.
> Billy didn't answer.
> That's how come I aint in uniform.
> Billy looked at the soldier. The soldier sat smoking.
> I tried to enlist, the barman said. Tried to lie about my age but they wasnt havin none of it.
> He dont care, the soldier said. Uniform dont mean nothin to him.
> The barman pulled on his cigarette and blew smoke toward the bar. I'll bet it'd mean somethin if it had been that risin sun on the collar and they was comin down Second Street about ten abreast. I bet it'd mean somethin then.

Think of dialogue in fiction as what is left when the extraneous verbiage is stripped away.

The repeated insult, *I bet it'd mean somethin then*, keeps the derogation and challenge in the air. The barman isn't allowing Billy to ignore him.

CONVEYING HESITATION OR HALTING SPEECH WITHOUT INTERJECTIONS

In the Watergate Tape Nixon and Haldeman intersperse their lines with "ah" or "uh," as we all do in real life. Don't be tempted to insert either of these empty interjections into your dialogue as a way of conveying hesitation or uncertainty. It's the easy way, but not the best one. Instead, write halting dialogue— dialogue that moves slowly, that *sounds* uncertain or groping. "Ah" and "uh" are clutter of the worst kind. Add "um" to that list of prohibited interjections and consider adding "hmm" as well. I say "consider" because some fine writers do use it in their dialogue, but "hmm" is a sound we make while we're thinking something over, and there are far better ways to convey a moment of reflection, as you'll see in chapter five.

How does it go, then, with no *uhs* or *ahs* or *ums*, when a character is thrown off balance, made hesitant? The boy, Bobby Guthrie, is undergoing a probing interrogation by the old woman, Mrs. Stearns in *Plainsong*:

> Who's your teacher?
> Miss Carpenter, Bobby said.
> I don't know her.
> She's got long hair and . . .
> And what? Mrs. Stearns said.
> She always wears sweaters.
> Does she.
> Mostly, he said.
> What do you know about sweaters?
> I don't know, Bobby said. I like them, I guess.

Bobby, flustered under this scrutiny, gives answers that grope without pausing. They aren't quite the right answers, and he knows it. The hesitation—*uh, ah*—is implicit. We can feel it in the marginal relevancy of Bobby's answers, and, especially, in the diction itself. It's slow. Try reading those lines, brief as they are, fast. You can't.

A good dialogue writer is a counterfeiter, fashioning currency that is more perfect than the real thing.

In *Play It As It Lays,* Didion puts the hesitancy of discomfort, and a loss for words, as much between the lines of the dialogue as in the words themselves in this colloquy between Maria Wyeth and her ex-husband, Carter. Maria has just found out she's pregnant:

> "You were afraid to call back about it." He was speaking in a careful monotone, a prosecutor with an open-and-shut case. "You thought if you didn't call back it would just go away."
>
> She closed her eyes. "I guess so. I guess that's right."
>
> "But now it's certain anyway. Otherwise the shot would have made you bleed."
>
> She nodded mutely.
>
> "What doctor. Who was the doctor."
>
> "Just a doctor. On Wilshire."
>
> "A doctor you didn't know. You thought that was smart."
>
> She said nothing.

Maria closes her eyes. She nods. She says nothing. Carter is pressing her, and she's having trouble shaping her responses. The answers, when they come, are uncertain and listless but never broken up with an interjection.

THE PARADOX OF GOOD DIALOGUE

Consider this biting colloquy from *Play It As It Lays*:

> "Listen to the music from the Kuliks'. They're having a party."
>
> "You going?"

"Of course I'm not going. He's a gangster."

"I just asked you if you were going to the party, Maria, I didn't ask for a grand-jury indictment." BZ paused. "In the second place he's not a gangster. He's a lawyer."

"For gangsters."

BZ shrugged. "I think of him more as a philosopher king. He told me once he understood the whole meaning of life, it came to him in a blinding flash one time when he almost died on the table at Cedars."

"Larry Kulik's not going to die at Cedars. Larry Kulik's going to die in a barber chair."

Few conversations in real life are this spare and incisive. A reviewer might praise dialogue as "realistic." It isn't, of course; it only sounds real to the ear of the reader. This is the paradox of dialogue in fiction: the better the dialogue, the less realistic it is likely to be, and the more realistic it will sound. Think of dialogue in fiction as what is left when the extraneous verbiage is stripped away. It is what we *mean* to say, what we *do* say, in essence. Think of your written dialogue as a form of shorthand that preserves the most vivid and succinct lines of an exchange or conversation. A reviewer described the dialogue in *The Friends of Eddie Coyle* as "so real it spits." It "spits" because of its intensity, the emotion compressed into every line. The dialogue in *Eddie Coyle* is so idiosyncratic, so colorful, so loaded, that its authenticity seems self-evident. It's evocative and compelling: how can it not be real? A good dialogue writer is a counterfeiter, fashioning currency that is more perfect than the real thing.

THE WRITER AS HOARDER—WHERE THE PICKINGS ARE GOOD

There's no one way to perform this trick of counterfeiting, once you've put aside real-life dialogue as your paradigm. You're on your own, with the opportunity—think of it as one—of creating a language that will seem so real it spits. It will be yours, and will mark you as a writer. There's no Esperanto in fictional dialogue; just as every writer has his or her own narrative voice, his or her characters have their own way of talking. Hemingway's dialogue is instantly recognizable. No one could confuse Anne Tyler's emotive dialogue with the wry plain-spoken speeches of Annie Proulx's characters. Joan Didion's dialogue is mordant and ironic, like her novels; Cormac McCarthy's dialogue is similarly edgy, but with more lilt and a frequent laconic note. Lee Smith's dialogue has a sprightliness, reflective of her resilient characters, and in it you can hear the soft accent of the Virginia hills.

Invent a spoken language—dialogue—that is a synthesis of what you read and what you hear, and that is appropriate to your characters and their time and place. Begin by reading good dialogue—lots of it—and noting how the words fall together. Study cadence, the ebb and flow of speeches, listening as you read. Hemingway's dialogue still has tracings in contemporary fiction. Cormac McCarthy now is influencing a generation of writers.

Listening to people talk is equally important, but the process here is different. You're a scavenger, a collector, picking up the bits and pieces that will enliven and enrich your dialogue: expressions, turns of phrase, slang, exclamations, the odd locution, the colorful solecism. Store them up; you never know when they'll come in handy.

In her 1972 interview with *The Paris Review*, Eudora Welty put it this way:

"Familiarity. Memory of the way things get said. Once you have heard certain expressions, sentences, you almost never forget them. It's like sending a bucket down the well and it always comes up full. You don't know you've remembered, but you have. And you listen for the right word, in the present, and you hear it. Once you're into a story everything seems to apply—what you overhear on a city bus is exactly what your character would say on the page you're writing. Wherever you go, you meet part of your story. I guess you're tuned in for it, and the right things are sort of magnetized—if you can think of your ears as magnets."

As a child I once heard someone say, "That's all well and good, but it don't feed the bulldog." It doesn't suffice, the man meant, and I understood that. I was planning to be a baseball player, not a writer, but the line, which struck me as interesting as well as funny, caught forever in my memory. Fifty years later, while I was writing *Seen the Glory*, it fell into the novel as if it had been waiting for just that moment. Lilac and Iris Purdy are identical twins, living alone on a farm in wartime Virginia and doing what they can to make ends meet. Here they are propositioning Thomas Chandler, a young Union soldier on picket duty:

"Y'all come back down tonight and bring four dollars. Two for each girl, you see."

Thomas swallowed. He roused himself and looked again at the woods and decided there was no one up there . . .

"I guess he ain't interested," one of the girls said.

"I might be," Thomas said.

"Might be don't feed the bulldog."

I have no idea if this is an old expression, or peculiar to the South. The man who said it in my presence wasn't southern, and for all I know it was his own invention. No matter. It had a rural and old-fashioned flavor. It was assertive. The twins are unlettered, but shrewd and plucky, and this sounded like them. It sounded *just* like them, no matter where it came from.

Listen to police officers, truck drivers, high school kids, ex-convicts, ballplayers, exotic dancers, social outcasts, debutantes, corporation presidents. Sort through their discourse and find the term, the phrase, the esoteric allusion that could be useful to you. Listen to politicians. If you heard Nixon and Haldeman in the Oval Office you might take note of Nixon's saying that Liddy isn't "too well screwed on," an unusual locution and oddly humorous. In Haldeman's parlance, news doesn't come from the CIA; it comes "from across the river." Good to know. Euphemisms are as useful in fiction as in real life. "Take this other step," Haldeman says, meaning flagrant suppression of evidence. He refers to the possible discovery of what they are up to, which would mean political disaster or worse, as "some directions we don't want this to go." Your characters, too, will resort to euphemism now and then.

Nixon sums up the machinations around him as "hanky-panky." One can imagine Joan Didion hearing the President of the United States using this quaint and unlikely word, and jotting it down in her memory—saving it for just the right moment, just the right character. The masseur "who wanted to be a writer" is whining in *Play It As It Lays:*

> "Don't be draggy, Helene, run down the beach and ask Audrey Wise for a couple of lemons. Ask Audrey and Jerry for Bloodys even. I mean we could definitely stand a few giggles."

Draggy, bloodys, a few giggles. The masseur is a poseur, and Didion uses words she heard somewhere, transposing them, to reveal his superficiality.

3

TENSION: SURPRISE IN EVERY LINE

The American Heritage Dictionary offers five definitions of tension, among them, "A strained relationship or barely controlled hostility between persons or groups," and "Uneasy suspense." These two meanings often fit the tension in fiction, but the concept is usually more subtle and hard to define. You might not even recognize it as tension, but if it weren't there, you'd miss it.

. . .

Tension is the substance of drama. The moment it disappears, your narrative turns slack. It becomes uninteresting. No matter what the conversation is about, no matter who is speaking to whom, no matter what the situation, tension must inhere in the dialogue, and it must be constant. If there's no tension in the scene you're writing, and if there's no way to create it, throw the scene out. It isn't helping your novel.

Suspense, minus the dictionary's "uneasy," gets close to the idea of tension in most dialogue. Suspense, in this loose definition, means not knowing what's coming. No line of dialogue should be easy to anticipate. Every line should contain some nugget of surprise.

Don't take this as a call for startling revelation every time a character speaks. The surprise in most dialogue is quiet; the point is unpredictability. Your characters cannot speak to each other, cannot respond to each other, in any easily assumable way. There has to be some wrinkle, some contradiction, some evasion, something of questionable relevance. Think of your characters as stage actors, playing off of each other. The audience at a play is in a state of suspense, in that it is wondering what's coming next. The moment that curiosity turns to indifference, the play stumbles. So does your novel.

No situation, however tranquil or steeped in good feeling, exempts you from the obligation to sustain the tension in your dialogue. A boy and girl sitting on a park bench, holding hands. A couple on their honeymoon, in a rowboat on a moonlit lake. A father tossing a baseball with his son. The idea of tension in moments like these seems counterintuitive, but if you need the scene you have to find the suspense in it—the dialogue that can't be anticipated, and that keeps us reading.

WHEN LOVERS TALK

Plainsong's Guthrie and his fellow teacher Maggie Smith run into each other at a dance in the Legion Hall. They already like each other, and they are in fine moods tonight:

> Maggie said, You better ask me to dance.
> You'd be taking a hell of a risk, Guthrie said.
> I know what I'm asking. I've seen you dance before.
> I can't imagine where that would've been.
> Here.
> Guthrie shook his head. That would've been a long time ago.
> It was. I've been watching you for a long time. Longer than you have any idea about.
> You're going to scare me now.
> I'm not scary, Maggie said. But I'm not a little girl either.
> I never thought you were, Guthrie said.
> Good. Then keep that in mind. Now ask me to dance.
> You're pretty sure of this?
> I'm very sure.

All right, Guthrie said. Would you care to dance, Mrs. Maggie Jones?

That's not very goddamn gallant, she said. But I guess it'll have to do.

It's a scene comprised of fun and incipient romance, but there's tension in every line. Maggie asks Guthrie to dance, and we know he's going to say yes—no suspense there. But the form the conversation takes—the verbal dance that precedes the actual one—is a playful joust which, in its archness and wit, gives the exchange its lovely tension.

They're playing off of each other, and we never know, from line to line, what the other is going to say. Guthrie's invitation, *Would you care to dance, Mrs. Maggie Jones?*, is framed in a faux and teasing formality which includes a nod to the fact that she, like him, was once married. Maggie's rejoinder—*That's not very goddamn gallant. But I guess it'll have to do*—bristles with sass and swagger, in counterpoint to Guthrie's sudden gallantry. There's tension in the contrast, and there's mutual delight. They're feeding each other good lines, challenging each other to respond in kind. Write a good line of dialogue—a smart one, a funny one—and you challenge yourself to write another.

Later Guthrie and Maggie find themselves in bed together:

Why, Maggie you look beautiful, Guthrie said. Don't you know that? You take the breath out of me.

Do you think so?

God, yes. Don't you know that? I thought you knew everything.

I know a lot, she said. But that's very nice to hear.

This is an earnest conversation, nothing like their playful banter at the dance, but again the tension is as constant. Maggie doesn't know how lovely she is, and, because she's so wise and self-assured, this surprises Guthrie—and the reader. A few moments later, Maggie is speaking:

> You don't actually think I'm scary, do you?
> Yeah, I do.
> Tell me the truth. I'm serious now.
> That is the truth. At times I can't say I know what to make of you.
> What do you mean? Why not?
> Because you're different than anyone else, he said. You don't seem to ever get defeated or scared by life. You stay clear in yourself, no matter what.
> She kissed him. Her dark eyes were watching him in the dim light. I get defeated sometimes, she said. I've been scared.

Suppose that, in answer to *You don't actually think I'm scary, do you?* Guthrie said, *No, of course not.* Maggie's interesting question would be settled to her satisfaction, and the tension would vanish. Having said yes, Guthrie has to explain himself: Maggie doesn't ever seem to get defeated or scared, he says. Maggie responds with a qualified admission: *I get defeated sometimes. I've been scared.* The speech is good *because* she qualifies it. She gets defeated *sometimes.* She's *been* scared, which doesn't mean she will be again. It isn't quite a flat denial, and that gives the line a slight, unpredictable twist. Maggie then reaches for Guthrie. Tension gone, scene over.

• • •

Dissimilarities between lovers are a natural source of tension in their dialogue—even the most trivial or insignificant differences. The protagonists and eventual lovers of my historical novel, *Little Bighorn*, are eighteen and sixteen. The year is 1876. Allen Winslow has had some sexual experience, Addie Grace Lord has had none:

> "I wonder you don't kiss me good night," she said.
> "I'm a gentleman."

"I wonder you don't try, even so."

"If I did you might slap me."

"I might. I might not."

"I don't want to risk it."

"I bet you've kissed a smart of girls," she said.

"I thought you were tired," he said.

"Well," she said, "if you're not interested . . ."

"You've been kissed plenty, I take it," he said.

"No," she said, "I've not."

"They must have wanted to," he said.

"None that I cared to be kissed by. Anyway, where was I to meet them? Chartwell's like a prison, as far as that goes."

"I thought you liked it there."

"I liked being away from Uncle Gordon, and don't change the subject."

Allen would indeed like to kiss her, and it wouldn't be out of character for him to suggest it, but there'd be no tension in the dialogue if it went that way. If she refused him, he wouldn't press her—it would be out of character—and the tension would be gone. I wanted them to kiss, but not without some tension leading up to it. The solution was to have the girl take the initiative and let the more worldly boy demur. Her forwardness surprises and amuses him; his coyness surprises *her*, and makes her a little bit indignant. Tension.

Whatever the situation, dialogue between lovers has a built-in tension that makes it some of the easiest dialogue to write. From the moment they notice each other, the two characters' mutual physical attraction adds an electric current to their dialogue. There's always something going on between lovers, at any stage in their relationship—some frisson of emotion that gives their dialogue a subtext, a meaning just beyond the literal. Characters in fiction take their lover's words to heart, as we do in real life. Every utterance matters. Angry words strike deep. Endearments whisper of things to come. Ambiguity charges innocuous-seeming words and phrases. Sexual tension is tension amplified. Give your lovers good lines, and you double your money.

KEEPING AN IMBALANCE BETWEEN FRIENDS

Tension in dialogue between friends, absent any physical attraction, may require a bit more thought and invention. Find the disparities between the characters—in temperament, outlook, opinion, background—and find ways to set these differences in opposition to each other—to dramatize them. Two best friends, John Grady Cole and Lacey Rawlins, are lying under the stars and talking in this low-key and comic scene in *All the Pretty Horses*:

> My daddy run off from home when he was fifteen. Otherwise I'd of been born in Alabama.
> You wouldnt of been born at all.
> What makes you say that?
> Cause your mama's from San Angelo and he never would of met her.
> He'd of met somebody.
> So would she.
> So?
> So you wouldnt of been born.
> I dont see why you say that. I'd of been born somewheres. How?
> Well why not?
> If your mama had a baby with her other husband and your daddy had one with his other wife which one would you be?
> I wouldnt be neither of em.
> That's right.
> Rawlins lay watching the stars. After a while he said: I could still be born. I might look different or somethin. If God wanted me to be born I'd be born.
> And if He didnt you wouldnt.

You're makin my goddamn head hurt.

I know it. I'm makin my own.

The argument here, if it can be called that, is character-driven. John Grady Cole is an existentialist, though he wouldn't know the term. Lacey Rawlins is literal-minded and stubborn, up to a point. McCarthy arranges a painless collision of the two intellects, dramatizing a difference that becomes crucial later on. The argument never becomes heated—there's affection in their unguardedness with each other—and yet the tension is constant. We have no idea what each will say next.

We have no idea, either, when young Sanders Roscoe comes to Sunday dinner in order to ask "old Raymond Pickett" for his daughter's hand in marriage in Haruf's *The Tie That Binds*. Sanders and Raymond adjourn to the parlor of the farmhouse after the meal:

After a time I said to him, "I suppose you know what I'm doing here."

"I see you got your tie on," he said. "I figured there was some reason for it."

"There is."

"More than just to eat Mavis's chicken dinner, you mean."

You understand the old son of a gun, that old wheat farmer, wasn't going to help me any. He was enjoying himself . . .

"That," I said. "And also to see what you thought of Mavis and me getting married."

"Tell the truth," he said, "I haven't given it much thought."

"Mavis has," I said.

"Has she, now?"

"Yes. Considerable."

"And what does she think about it?"

"She's in favor of it."

"But you ain't said nothing about yourself yet. Most times I believe it takes two to get married."

> "Oh, I don't mind," I said.
>
> "Well, now," he said, looking at me. "She's in favor and you say you don't mind. I guess that'll have to do, won't it?"

Raymond now changes the subject—his Sunday shoes are hurting him. He recalls seeing Sanders's late father at farm sales. Then:

> "Well, now. About this marriage business—it sounds like Mavis has her mind all made up."
>
> I nodded.
>
> "She's like that. So I don't see where it would do me much good to object even if I wanted to. Can you?"
>
> "No."
>
> "I thought as much. Well, it's nice having girls in the house. I believe I'll miss that."

Each line of this dry colloquy takes us pleasantly by surprise. You can't see it coming. We know Raymond Pickett is going to say yes to the marriage, but "the old wheat farmer" is amusing himself, and there's no predicting how long he'll do this, or what twists the conversation will take. We read on, to find out.

Even though the subject is the suicide of an elderly woman in T. R. Pearson's *A Short History of a Small Place,* this interview by "Miss Bambi Kinch of Action News Five" with the local sheriff is a treat for everyone who picks up the novel:

> "Who is the victim, sheriff?" she asked him.
>
> "Well, Bambi," the sheriff said and hooked his thumbs in his front beltloops, "the victim is a female caucasian, approximately sixty-five years of age."
>
> "Was she a resident of Neely?"
>
> "Well, Bambi, yes she was an indigenous native."
>
> "Do you suspect foul play, sheriff?"

"Well, Bambi, at this point we think it's a suicide brought on probably by moral derangement."

"Did she have a history of this sort of thing?"

"Well, Bambi, not that we know of. She's never done this before."

Bambi's questions are comically—and surprisingly—unimaginative, and the sheriff is in over his head and doesn't know it. He prefaces every answer with a pompous and self-conscious *Well, Bambi,* and as the repetitions accumulate they become more and more unlikely—he *can't* keep saying it, we think—and funnier and funnier. It's tension that makes us smile.

WHEN THE TENSION IS HIGH

And then there's open hostility, which simplifies things for the writer. Quarrels and confrontations are relatively easy to write; there's nothing subtle about the dialogue, nothing veiled or indirect. But the stricture against the predictable line still applies. Your characters shouldn't know what's coming any more than the reader does. They should keep each other off balance.

Ernest Hemingway's famous short story, *The Killers,* was published in 1927, and the dialogue might have been written yesterday. Two gangsters, Al and Max, come into a small-town diner at suppertime and tie up the cook and young Nick Adams in the kitchen. Al sticks a shotgun through the opening where food is passed to the front. Max and George, the owner of the diner, are at the counter:

"Talk to me, bright boy," Max said. "What do you think's going to happen?"

George did not say anything.

"I'll tell you," Max said. "We're going to kill a Swede. Do you know a big Swede named Ole Andreson?"

"Yes."

"He comes in here to eat every night, don't he?"

"Sometimes he comes here."

"He comes here at six o'clock, don't he?"

"If he comes."

"We know all that, bright boy," Max said. "Talk about something else. Ever go to the movies?"

"Once in a while."

"You ought to go the movies more. The movies are fine for a bright boy like you."

"What are you going to kill Ole Andreson for? What did he ever do to you?"

"He never had a chance to do anything to us. He never even seen us."

"And he's only going to see us once," Al said from the kitchen.

"What are you going to kill him for, then?" George asked.

"We're killing him for a friend. Just to oblige a friend, bright boy."

"Shut up," said Al from the kitchen. "You talk too goddamn much."

There are twelve speeches here, and none is more than two sentences long. The short speeches keep the interaction going with no letup, sustaining the tension from moment to moment. Short speeches keep both sides in the game. Don't give characters any breathing space. They need to react, not think; don't give them time.

A sinister stranger accosts Billy Parham, who is still a boy, and his younger brother, near their ranch in the opening pages of *The Crossing:*

Howdy, said Billy.

The Indian spat. Spooked everything in the country, aint you? he said.

We didn't know there was anybody here.

You aint got nothin to eat?

No sir.

Where you live at?

About two miles down the river.

You got anything to eat at your house?

Yessir.

I come down there you goin to bring me somethin out?

You can come to the house. Mama'll feed you.

I don't want to come to the house. I want you to bring me somethin out.

All right.

You goin to bring me somethin out?

Yes.

All right then.

Again, short speeches keep the tension incessant. The Indian's lines drip with menace. Billy is trying to propitiate him, but the Indian **Short speeches keep the tension** won't let him out of the conversation. Billy is caught in it, and has to return line for line, with no time to collect himself. The speeches in this exchange, like those above in *The Killers,* are never more than a sentence or two long.

There's no menace in this Sunday dinner scene from Ernest J. Gaines's *A Lesson Before Dying*, but the hostility is overt, nevertheless. The narrator and protagonist, a schoolteacher named Grant Wiggins, has brought his girlfriend, Vivian, home for the first time. Grant lives with his formidable aunt, and she starts right in on Vivian:

"You go to church?"

"I'm Catholic."

My aunt looked at Vivian and nodded her head, as if she was thinking, What else could you possibly be?

"You went to church today?"

"I went to nine o'clock mass," Vivian said.

"You going next Sunday?"

"Yes, ma'am."

"Sunday after that?"

"I hope so."

"This one," my aunt said, nodding toward me but still looking at Vivian, "he don't have a church. What y'all go'n do then?"

"We'll work it out," Vivian said.

""You go'n leave your church?"

"I hope I don't have to," Vivian said.

This is an inquisition, and Vivian doesn't flinch from it. Her answers are courteous, but they aren't the answers Grant's aunt is looking for. The aunt presses the inquisition, Vivian remains unruffled. She answers truthfully, unapologetically, standing her ground. The tension never flags.

KEEPING THE SUSPENSE IN MONOLOGUES

Tension eases when a character holds the floor for a while, but it shouldn't disappear. Hold on to the notion of "suspense," and write monologues that not only surprise us, but keep us wanting to know what's coming next. No one will ever write anything equal to Shakespeare's soliloquies, but their power to cast a spell— to draw us in and keep us engaged, as a matter of both pleasure and curiosity—is the gold standard. Dennis Lenahan, the high diver in Elmore Leonard's *Tishomingo Blues*, is no Lear, but he can grab our attention and hold it. The target of his dives is a twenty-foot-wide tank eighty feet below. He's applying for a job as an entertainer at a resort casino here:

"I've got eighty dives from different heights and most of 'em I can do hungover, like a flying reverse somersault, your standard high dive. But I don't know what I'm gonna do till I'm up there. It depends on the crowd, how the show's going. But I'll tell you something, you stand on the perch looking down eighty feet to the water, you know you're alive."

We don't know what a flying reverse somersault is, but we know Dennis performs it through eighty feet of air, into a small tank, and that is enough to stir our imagination and pull us into the circus-like drama of Dennis Lenahan's profession. The fourth and last sentence tells us all we need to know about why Dennis is a diver.

Dave Foley, the federal agent in *The Friends of Eddie Coyle*, has taken an interest in a rumor he's been hearing about Eddie. He talks about it to a pal in law enforcement:

"You remember Eddie Fingers," Dave said. "Eddie Coyle? Fellow got his hand busted up after they put Billy Wallace away for a long time on a gun that he bought from somebody. Got himself in a whole mess of trouble up in New Hampshire trucking a little booze that didn't belong to him about this time last year."

Foley and Dennis Lenahan, the high diver, are entertaining characters whose dialogue is textured by their professions. Dennis's monologue is self-promoting and full of swagger, with an affected nonchalance—the daredevil talking. Foley's monologue is laconic, deadpan. It's cop talk. Neither repeats himself, or wanders off subject. We never know what's coming next.

Atticus Finch, the small-town defense attorney and hero of Harper Lee's iconic novel of bigotry and moral courage, *To Kill a Mockingbird*, delivers a very different sort of monologue in his summation in the trial of Tom Robinson, the black man accused of raping a white girl:

"But there is one way in this country in which all men are created equal—there is one human institution that makes a pauper the equal of a Rockefeller, the stupid man the equal of an

Einstein, and the ignorant man the equal of any college president. That institution, gentlemen, is a court. It can be the Supreme Court of the United States or the humblest J.P. court in the land, or this honorable court which you serve. Our courts have their faults, as does any human institution, but in this country our courts are our great levelers, and in our courts all men are created equal.

"I'm no idealist to believe firmly in the integrity of our courts and in the jury system—that is no ideal to me, it is a living, working reality. Gentlemen, a court is no better than each man of you sitting before me on this jury. A court is only as sound as its jury, and a jury is only as sound as the men who make it up. I am confident that you gentlemen will review without passion the evidence you have heard, come to a decision, and restore this defendant to his family. In the name of God, do your duty."

It's one of literature's signal speeches, for obvious reasons. Note its economy. Look for a word or phrase that you could cut without losing anything; you can't find it. Suspense keeps us reading—that constant unpredictability, that lurking surprise. *What comes next?* If it's an empty word, an unnecessary one, the monologue stalls, the tension vanishes.

4

HEARING IS SEEING

How soon after entering the novel does an important character speak? Do we need to hear him or her in those first moments? Where do dialogue and physical description converge in the creation of the outward character?

Captain Ahab finally appears on page 120 of the Modern Library edition of *Moby Dick*, after several days of wondering and speculation among the crew:

> There seemed no sign of common bodily illness about him, nor of the recovery of any. He looked like a man cut away from the stake, when the fire has overrunningly wasted all the limbs without consuming them, or taking away one particle from their compacted age and robustness. His whole high, broad, form seemed made of solid bronze, and shaped in an unalterable mould, like Cellini's cast Perseus. Threading its way out from among the grey hairs, and continuing right down one side of his tawny scorched face and neck, till it disappeared in his clothing, you saw a slender rod-like mark, lividly whitish. It resembled that perpendicular seam sometimes made in the straight, lofty trunk of a great tree, when the upper lightning tearingly darts down it, and without wrenching a single twig, peels and grooves out the

bark from top to bottom ere running off into the soil, leaving the tree still greenly alive, but branded . . . So powerfully did the whole grim aspect of Ahab affect me, and the livid brand which streaked it, that for the first few moments I hardly noted that not a little bit of this overbearing grimness was owing to the barbaric white leg upon which he stood.

Frederic Henry gets his first look at Catherine Barkley on page 18 of *A Farewell to Arms*:

Miss Barkley was quite tall. She wore what seemed to me to be a nurse's uniform, was blond and had tawny skin and gray eyes. I thought she was very beautiful.

Two great novels, two very different approaches to the physical description of a major character. Hemingway gives us a little help, then lets our imagination do the rest. Melville paints Ahab down to the last wrinkle. How much physical description to write, if any, is a decision you make every time a character walks into your novel. How much of the portrait do you want to leave to the reader's imagination, and how does that work? How, with little or no physical description, do you create a character's image in the reader's mind's eye?

VOICE AS PHYSICAL DESCRIPTION

Huckleberry Finn is one of the most enduringly vivid characters in all of literature, and yet there isn't a word of description of him anywhere in the novel. In all of *Moby Dick*, Ishmael never tells us what he looks like. Few first-person narrators do. Scour what is perhaps Faulkner's greatest novel, *The Sound and the Fury*, for a physical description of any member of the Compson family, and, amazingly, you won't find it. Why, then, do we see Huck, Ishmael, and the Compsons so clearly?

Benjy Compson, the idiot, is the narrator of the unforgettable first section of the novel:

> I listened to the water.
>
> I couldn't hear the water, and Caddy opened the door.
>
> "Why, Benjy," she said. She looked at me and I went and she put her arms around me. "Did you find Caddy again," she said. "Did you think Caddy had run away." Caddy smelled like trees.
>
> We went to Caddy's room. She sat down at the mirror. She stopped her hands and looked at me.
>
> "Why, Benjy. What is it," she said. "You mustn't cry. Caddy's not going away. See here," she said. She took up the bottle and took the stopper out and held it to my nose. "Sweet. Smell. Good."
>
> I went away and I didn't hush, and she held the bottle in her hand, looking at me.
>
> "Oh," she said. She put the bottle down and came and put her arms around me. "So that was it. And you were trying to tell Caddy and you couldn't tell her. You wanted to, but you couldn't, could you. Of course Caddy wont. Just wait till I dress."

Benjy's simple-mindedness and confusion—he doesn't hear questions as questions—are captured in his narrative voice, and so are the hurt and sensitivity that no one but Caddy perceives, or even tries to perceive. Bewilderment, anguish, muddled longing: with this welter of emotions comes the visible person. Faulkner has tripped our imagination. We see the pain in Benjy's eyes, a tragic confusion of loss and fright.

Caddy's dialogue in this scene brims with compassion, and we also hear her fearlessness in displaying it. There's love in her words to her pathetic brother. Earlier in the novel—the action in the first two sections of *The Sound and the Fury* shifts erratically here and there in time—a younger Caddy reveals her venturesome side. Benjy is remembering:

> We were playing in the branch and Caddy squatted down and got her dress wet and Versh said,
>
> "Your mommer going to whip you for getting your dress wet."
>
> "She's not going to do any such thing," Caddy said.
>
> "How do you know," Quentin said.
>
> "That's all right how I know," Caddy said. "How do you know."
>
> "She said she was," Quentin said. "Besides, I'm older than you."
>
> "I'm seven years old," Caddy said. "I guess I know."
>
> "I'm older than that," Quentin said. "I go to school. Don't I, Versh."
>
> "I'm going to school next year," Caddy said.
>
> "You know she whip you when you get your dress wet," Versh said.
>
> "It's not wet," Caddy said. She stood up in the water and looked at her dress. "I'll take it off," she said. "Then it'll dry."
>
> "I bet you won't," Quentin said.
>
> "I bet I will," Caddy said.
>
> "I bet you better not," Quentin said.
>
> Caddy came to Versh and me and turned her back.
>
> "Unbutton it, Versh," she said.

There's high spirit in Caddy's every line here, the headstrong quality that we can only admire, but which will lead to so much grief later on. Faulkner never tells us she's pretty, but we know she is, from her airy boldness, her self-assurance. This is a girl who's comfortable in her own skin, knows admiration will come her way and is indifferent when it doesn't. She's obviously smart. Her dialogue is so alive that we can't help but see her without ever reading a word of physical description.

In the fourth and final section of the novel, when the Compsons' doughty and long-suffering servant, Dilsey, takes her family and Benjy to the Easter service at her ramshackle Baptist church, Faulkner describes the two ministers, who appear nowhere else in the novel—their size, complexions, physiognomies, attire. Why describe minor characters and not major ones? Faulkner, clearly, prefers to let his greatest characters come alive in the wide world of the reader's imagination.

McCarthy, Higgins, and Didion work this way. Higgins tells us that Eddie Coyle is "stocky," and our imagination takes over from there. Higgins never tells us what Foley and Jackie Brown look like. We know Maria Wyeth is pretty because she's an actress, but her face and figure are evoked entirely in her dialogue.

• • •

In his acclaimed short story, *A Small, Good Thing*, Raymond Carver gives us the baker's small eyes and "bristly flesh around his cheeks" and lets the his dialogue fill out the picture:

> "You want to pick up your three-day old cake? That it? I don't want to argue with you, lady. There it sits over there, getting stale. I'll give it to you for half of what I quoted you. No. You want it? You can have it. It's no good to me, no good to anyone now. It cost me time and money to make that cake. If you want it, okay, if you don't, that's okay, too. I have to get back to work."

The baker doesn't know that the woman and her husband didn't pick up their little boy's cake because the boy was run over and killed. The baker, in a malicious pique, has been telephoning Ann and Howard at all hours, harassing them, and they've come to the bakery in the middle of the night to confront him. Their news, and their grief, leaves him thunderstruck and, after a moment, a changed man:

> "God alone knows how sorry I am. Listen to me. I'm just a baker. I don't claim to be anything else. Maybe once, maybe years ago, I was different kind of human being. I've forgotten, I don't

know for sure. But I'm not any longer, if I ever was. Now I'm just a baker. That don't excuse my doing what I did, I know. But I'm deeply sorry. I'm sorry for your son, and I'm sorry for my part in this," the baker said. He spread his hands on the table and turned them over to reveal his palms . . . "You understand what it comes down to is I don't know how to act anymore, it would seem. Please," the man said, "let me ask you if you can find it in your hearts to forgive me?"

These are the words, ill-humored and vindictive in the first speech, stricken with remorse and self-loathing in the second, of a sad, failed, lonely man. An image comes to mind—a face, a physiognomy. To hear this man is to see him.

EVOKING FACIAL EXPRESSION

There are only so many ways to write facial expression. There's smiling, grinning, smirking, glowering, glaring. There are raised eyebrows, widened eyes, a wrinkled or furrowed forehead. Eyes can bug out, though I'd be careful with that one. There's the quizzical look. There's the frown.

All of these ways of showing the reader your characters' faces at important moments have their limitations. They're generic; they lack specificity and nuance. Yes, your characters are going to have to smile and grin, but too many smiles can wear the verb out, till one smile becomes just like any other. As for smirks, I would limit myself to one or two per novel. It's a good verb but a conspicuous one, and you reduce its effect when you overuse it, as you do with smiles. And how many times can characters glare or glower at one another before the action becomes trite? The nature of a frown depends on the character—Ahab's frown is screwed permanently into his lowering, weathered face; Daisy Buchanan's is fleeting, quickly wiped away by her natural verve and radiance.

There's a way around the limited vocabulary of facial expressions: dialogue. There isn't much nuance in a frown, a raised eyebrow, or widened eyes, but dialogue can be infinitely nuanced and supple. It can express any mood, any emotion, subtle or blatant, and make it visible in the landscape of the human face.

Lee Smith is very good at freighting her dialogue with sly sexual tension, and she writes lively first encounters between men and women. Her heroines are regularly bewitched by smooth-talking charmers, some of them scoundrels, some not. Molly Petree, the protagonist of *On Agate Hill*, is smitten by the banjo player, Jacky Jarvis, one night at a log cabin dance in the North Carolina hill country. Smith gives us a good look at Jacky when he enters the dance, and the novel. The year is 1883. Molly is narrating:

> He appeared to have no bones at all in his body. He was tall and skinny with yellow-red hair that fell forward into his eyes and a big nose and a wide crooked reckless grin, the kind of a face that you couldn't quit looking at . . . He was the kind of man that made everybody feel better just because he had walked into the room.

Jackie's physiognomy is pronounced and suggestive, but it is his dialogue that captures his appeal and animates the odd, plain face:

> I stood back in the trees away from the fire and sipped at the cup. My hair was falling all down my back and my blouse was wet clear through from dancing.
>
> "My name is Jacky Jarvis," he said into my ear, "and I've been looking for you all my life."
>
> I whirled around. "That's a lie," I cried. "You never even heard of me before." His breath on my neck gave me the shivers.
>
> "But I been dreaming about you every night," he said. "So I knowed you right off. Maybe I just dreamed you up." His face was

real close to mine, he was grinning such a wide devil-may-care grin that he made me dizzy.

"Oh, is that a fact?" I said, stepping back from him. "Well, too bad, you're too late." I held up my hand and my ring caught the firelight, winking at him.

He gave a long low whistle through his teeth. "Mighty fine ring," he said. "Who is the lucky feller?"

"Nobody you know."

"Maybe, maybe not," he said, looking at me.

"Molly!" Martha called, peering across the fire. "Come on, honey, we've got to go."

He touched my elbow. "Listen. I'm coming to see you tomorrow."

"You are not," I said. "You haven't been invited. You don't know where I live. You don't even know who I am."

He smiled out from under the brim of his hat. "I'll find out. I'll give you your own private music show."

"Molly," Martha was calling.

I turned to go, then turned back. "Don't come tomorrow," I said. "Come Sunday."

Jacky's sincerity is suspect at this point, but in his seduction of Molly his face comes alive in the reader's mind's eye. Jacky's grinning, but the verb is hardly necessary: you can *see* the grin in his dialogue. And it's not a generic grin—the dialogue clarifies, distinguishes it, makes it Jacky's own.

And don't miss Molly's obviously feigned disinterest, which gives the exchange its wonderful tension. Molly doesn't describe her own face, of course, but we can see, in her dialogue, the prim mouth, the upturned chin, and something more—in the eyes, perhaps, which tell us, and tell Jacky Jarvis, that Molly's coolness is an act. Her exit line is spoken low and hastily—the dialogue can be read no other way—and Molly shoots Jacky a glance stripped of all coyness and pretense. She doesn't tell us that, but it's there, visible, in five words of dialogue.

The more blatant emotions—dislike, anger, disgust—are easy. "I despise you," Ellen said—no need to tell us she glared at Mike when she said it; the glare is in the dialogue. *I despise you:* the face is set, eyes narrowed. Suppose we dress the line up a little, give it a more distinctive flavor: *I despise everything you stand for.* The voice comes down, it's quieter but no less adamant, and Ellen's expression hardens, turns steely, judgmental. It's all in her dialogue.

Ahab's madness has a firmer grip on him when he addresses the crew again on the deck of the *Pequod:*

> "Aye, aye! and I'll chase him round Good Hope, and round the Horn, and round the Norway Maelstrom, and round perdition's flames before I give him up. And this is what ye have shipped for, men! to chase that white whale on both sides of land, and over all sides of earth, till he spouts black blood and rolls fin over. What say ye, men, will ye splice hands on it, now?"

Melville's dialogue, by any modern standard, is baroque and overwrought, which makes it tailor-made for Ahab. In this speech we see the wildness in his eyes, the feverish animation flaring in the face. There's no way to make a face this expressive except with dialogue.

Mark Twain, speaking to us in the voice of Huckleberry Finn, puts the camera on Huck's vagabond father when he enters the novel early on. He has sneaked into Huck's bedroom in the Widow Douglas's house late at night, and Huck finds him waiting for him:

> He was most fifty, and he looked it. His hair was long and tangled and greasy, and hung down, and you could see his eyes shining through like he was behind vines. It was all black, no gray; so was his long, mixed-up whiskers. There warn't no color in his face, where his face showed; it was white; not like another man's white,

but a white to make a body sick, a white to make a body's flesh crawl—a tree-toad white, a fish-belly white. As for his clothes—just rags, that was all.

No other character in the novel is described at such length; it isn't close. Why? We can only assume Twain thought that Huck's "Pap" is filthy, ragged, and dissipated beyond our capacity to imagine him. Twain burns his image onto our mind's eye and, from here on, lets Pap's dialogue show us the face in all its tortured moods. In this first appearance he lights into Huck without preamble:

"Starchy clothes—very. You think you're a good deal of a big-bug, don't you?"

"Maybe I am, maybe I ain't," I says.

"Don't give me none o' your lip," says he. "You've put on considerable many frills since I been away. I'll take you down a peg before I get done with you. You're educated, too, they say—can read and write. You think you're better'n your father, now, don't you, because he can't? I'll take it out of you. Who told you might meddle with such hifalut'n foolishness, hey?—who told you could?"

Pap's rant is a snarl; to hear the snarl is to see it on the ravaged face. It would be hard to think of a character more different from Huck's depraved father than Atticus Finch, whose image comes entirely from his dialogue. Atticus is so vivid that one can read all of *To Kill a Mockingbird* without realizing that Harper Lee never tells us what he looks like. As a loving father and courageous courtroom defender of Tom Robinson, Atticus is subject to moods and emotions of the most profound sort, and we see them all in his face, which is somber, gentle, and strong, all at once. The novel is narrated by Atticus's twelve-year-old daughter, Jean Louise, who goes by "Scout." Early in the book Scout asks Atticus why the poor and disreputable Bob Ewell is allowed to hunt out of season:

"It's against the law, all right," said my father, "and it's certainly bad, but when a man spends his relief checks on green whiskey his children have a way of crying from hunger pains. I don't know of any landowner around here who begrudges those children any game their father can hit."

"Mr. Ewell shouldn't do that—"

"Of course he shouldn't, but he'll never change his ways. Are you going to take out your disapproval on his children?"

This is the compassionate Atticus, proponent of simple, bedrock morals. He's wise. He's patient. We see the facial expression in the dialogue.

And there is this line near the end of the novel, after Boo Radley has saved Jem and Scout from being murdered, committing murder himself on the dark path through the woods on Halloween night:

> Before he went inside the house, he stopped in front of Boo Radley. "Thank you for my children, Arthur," he said.

It's one of the most powerful moments in the novel, and one of the most vivid. Atticus's six words are a close-up: a good man, shaken but collected, deeply grateful. The line survives intact in the movie; we see Gregory Peck's expressive face close up as he speaks it, but if you've read the book, you've been here already.

FILM DIALOGUE VS. DIALOGUE ON THE PAGE

Take two novels that were written first as screenplays: *On the Waterfront*, by Budd Schulberg (the novel is *Waterfront*), and McCarthy's *No Country For Old Men*. In both cases, particularly *No Country For Old Men*, much of the dialogue was moved straight from script to novel.

It usually happens the opposite way, of course—book first, then the movie based on it. When the book is good—*The Maltese Falcon, To Kill a Mockingbird, The Friends of Eddie Coyle, Lonesome Dove*—the screenplay writer alters the story little, if at all, and helps himself liberally to the dialogue.

My point? Good dialogue in fiction, as in *To Kill a Mockingbird* or *Eddie Coyle,* translates effectively to the screen. It can't be improved upon, whether read or spoken. But you wouldn't watch *To Kill a Mockingbird* to help you with the dialogue in your novel; you'd read Harper Lee's great book. Better to read *No Country For Old Men* than to watch it, for instruction in writing dialogue; there's more of it, for one thing, and how it works on the page is your concern.

You won't learn how to write good dialogue by watching movies.

But should you watch a film from an original screenplay to help you with the dialogue in your novel? I'm going to challenge a widely held assumption and say no. I'll put it this way: listen to people talk in the movies the same way you listen in real life, noting the useful term, expression, or turn of phrase. You won't learn how to write good dialogue by watching movies any more than you will by listening to the conversation at dinner tonight.

Screenplay writers have it a lot easier than we novelists do. For one thing, they have directors and cameramen to spell out action for them—to tell a character how to move, how to stand. For another, they have actors speaking their lines. Actors are their intermediaries, positioned to interpret the dialogue—to give it tone, texture, color, nuance—as they choose, or are told to do. A good actor can turn a bland line pungent. He can inject humor into a line that isn't intrinsically funny. He can turn a banal line sorrowful. Actors use their voices, and—in film, especially—their faces, and screenplay writers, naturally, rely on them. Think of Marlon Brando as the motorcycle rebel in *The Wild Ones,* or the mafia don, Vito Corleone, in *The Godfather*—of the eloquence in his face as he speaks.

I think it's safe to say that *On the Waterfront,* the film, is better than the novel it became, *Waterfront.* A lot better, actually. Today the novel is largely forgotten, but the movie remains a classic, rated the eighth best American film of all time by the American Film Institute.

One of its best known scenes takes place in the dark back seat of a car, a conversation between the mobster, Charley "the Gent" Malloy, played by Rod Steiger, and his younger brother Terry, the ex-prizefighter, played by Brando. Charley has been ordered by his boss to dissuade Terry, by threat or the inducement of a cushy job, from testifying against the syndicate. Terry balks, and Charley, desperate, pulls a gun on his brother. From the novel:

> When Terry saw the gun in the folds of the overcoat, he was not frightened; the shock of this final gesture seemed to carry him beyond fear into a state of stunned, intuitive compassion he had never known before.
>
> "Charley . . ." he said sadly, embarrassed for both of them. He reached out and gently turned the barrel to one side.
>
> Charley leaned back against the seat and lowered the gun into his lap. He pushed his hat back to let his forehead breathe. He took an initialed handkerchief out of his breast pocket and mopped his face.
>
> "Please take it," Charley whispered. "Please take that job."
>
> Terry had pulled away into his corner of the back seat. He was still shaking his head in shock and disappointment. "Charley—oh, Charley." A deep sigh welled out of him that said, "Wow . . ."

Charley's line here is pretty good—you can hear the agony in it; not for himself but for Terry—but Terry's lines, which come straight from the movie, might better have been left there. *Charley—oh, Charley*—there's "shock" and "disappointment" in the line only because Schulberg tells us there is. Without the author's direction, the line could be read in a variety of ways. It could be spoken lovingly. It's a line that doesn't speak for itself; it needs help. Rewrite Terry's line as an exercise. Write a line that *creates* shock and disappointment, makes them visible in the speaker's face.

Terry then sighs, and it isn't quite clear whether he says, "Wow," as he does, memorably, in the movie, or whether "Wow" is only the sigh's import, a translation of it. Either way, with all due respect to Budd Schulberg, I would advise you to be circumspect, at the very least, about using "wow" in your dialogue. Its commonness works against it, for one thing, and its multiple inspirations in real life. A child might say it at a circus, or a husband upon seeing his wife in a new evening dress. You might say it in reaction to a long jump shot or a fifty-yard pass. It's a generic interjection that isn't likely to surprise the reader. It's hard to imagine McCarthy, Haruf, Higgins, Didion, or Dorothy Parker using it. It's impossible to imagine one of Hemingway's or Faulkner's characters saying "wow."

And yet the word, coming after *Charley—oh, Charley*, comprises one of filmdom's most memorable lines. The difference, of course, is Marlon Brando. Brando turns those four ordinary words, ending with *Wow*, into a soft wail of anguish, using his face *and* his voice, cramming the line with emotion called straight from Terry Malloy's breaking heart.

There's no better illustration than this of the difference between dialogue in film and fiction. The screenplay writer has actors, and you never do. You don't have Brando, Paul Newman, or Meryl Streep to give visible eloquence to your dialogue, to interpret it for you. It's up to you. Your dialogue should evoke a character physically, as I've said, and it should convey, as well, the look on his or her face as the lines are spoken. The emotion in the dialogue should find expression in the face. Pain, joy, wonderment, disgust: we should *see* them.

Here are two prime examples of expressive dialogue:

John Grady Cole, in *Cities of the Plain,* asks Billy Parham to do him a surprising favor. The conversation goes on awhile, and you can pick it up anywhere and watch the two boys' faces as they talk, sitting alone in the rear of a bar in the afternoon quiet:

Let me see if I got this straight. You want me to go to a whorehouse in Juarez Mexico and buy this whore cash money and bring her back across the river to the ranch. Is that about the size of it?

John Grady nodded.

Shit, said Billy. Smile or somethin, will you? Goddamn. Tell me you aint gone completely crazy.

I aint gone completely crazy.

The hell you aint.

I'm in love with her, Billy.

Billy slumped back in his chair. His arms hung uselessly by his side. Aw goddamn, he said. Goddamn.

I cant help what it sounds like.

My own damn fault. I never should of took you down there. Never in this world. It's my fault. Hell, I don't even know what I'm complainin about.

He leaned and took his lighted cigarette from the tin ashtray where he'd put it and took a pull on it and blew the smoke across the table. Tell me this, he said.

All right.

What in the goddamn hell would you do with her if you did get her away from down there? Which you aint.

Marry her.

Billy paused with the cigarette half way to his mouth. He put it down again.

Well, that's it, he said. That's it. I'm havin your ass committed.

John Grady's expression, which we see in his short, quiet answers, never changes. We see his gaze, downcast or averted. Billy's face is animated. Another writer might tell us that his eyes widen, or that he grimaces, or scrunches his face (avoid this last one). McCarthy uses only dialogue, and we see a kaleidoscope of emotions in the young cowboy's sunbrowned face: incredulity, worry, exasperation, and, at times, a blend of all three. You can't bring all of that to a character's face except with dialogue.

The human face doesn't get any more stricken than Nat Turner's and his friend Hark's on the searing next-to-last page of William Styron's masterful historical novel, *The Confessions of Nat Turner*. Nat was the leader of the 1831 slave rebellion in Virginia, and we are now in the drafty little jail where Nat and Hark have spent their final days:

> In a long drawn-out breath Hark's wail dies away. Now I hear a hurried sound of snapping ropes as they tie him into the chair. Then the white men whisper and grunt while they strain beneath the weight of their burden and lift Hark out into the hallway. Shadows leap up and quiver in the lantern's brassy radiance. The white men shuffle in furious labor, gasping with the effort. Hark's bound and seated shape, like the silhouette of some marvelous black potentate borne in stately procession toward his throne, passes slowly by my door. I reach out as if to touch him, feel nothing, clutch only a handful of air.
>
> "Dis yere some way to go," I hear Hark say. "Good-bye, ole Nat!" he calls.
>
> "Good-bye, Hark," I whisper, "good-bye, good-bye."
>
> "Hit gwine be all right, Nat," he cries out to me, the voice fading. "Ev'ythin gwine be all right! Dis yere ain't nothin', Nat, nothin' atall. Good-bye, ole Nat, good-bye."

Exclamation points granted, and no actor needed.

5

CHOREOGRAPHY AND DESCRIPTION AND THEIR RELATIONSHIP TO DIALOGUE

Good dialogue conveys facial expression, but what about the speaker's posture, movements, gestures—the choreography? What is he doing while he's talking, and how important is it that the reader sees him doing it?

It depends, of course, on the circumstances. A dinner conversation needs little choreography, and there isn't much available—a glass lifted, a waiter summoned, food pushed around on a plate. There isn't much Charley and Terry Malloy can do, sitting in the back seat of the car with their arms folded. There's more freedom, say, on a park bench; your two characters might lean forward, or slump back, as they talk. They might watch a woman go by, or look up into the trees. If your characters are standing on the field at Yankee Stadium during batting practice, they're paying at least some attention to what's going on around them as they talk. Their gazes are going to shift. They might hear a shout from the grandstand and glance over there. If they're in a bar, they're drinking, and the reader should see them doing it. Does she gingerly raise a stemmed martini glass? Is he slugging beer out of the bottle?

There are two reasons, which often coincide, to interrupt your dialogue with a gesture or action. The first is to hold on to the character visually—to keep him or her clearly in front of us.

The second is to create a pause, to clarify the moment or enhance its dramatic effect.

INTERRUPTING DIALOGUE TO KEEP A CHARACTER'S PHYSICAL APPEARANCE FRONT AND CENTER

This can be important when the character is unusual physically—when physical makeup is crucial to who the character is. Ahab, with his hard-set, weathered face and wooden leg, is an example of this, and Melville keeps his image before us. Fitzgerald flashes constantly on Daisy Buchanan, whose character and sprightly beauty are inextricable. No one can forget, for a moment, what Ahab and Daisy look like. Powerhouse, the obese pianist and protagonist of Eudora Welty's brilliant short story of the same name, is noteworthy in his appearance, to put it mildly:

> He has pale gray eyes, heavy lids, maybe horny like a lizard's, but big glowing eyes when they're open . . . There he is with his great head, fat stomach, and little round piston legs, and long yellow-sectioned strong big fingers, at rest about the size of bananas.

The story gathers around Powerhouse as he performs in a roadhouse, then goes across the street with his band during intermission to drink a beer. His dialogue is compulsive and incessant, and amounts to a second narrative voice, and Welty keeps reminding us, as he talks, how emphatically this immense and compelling figure fills space. He is conversing with his musicians as they play at the white dance in this small Mississippi town far from their home:

> "Aaaaaaaaa!" shouts Powerhouse, flinging out both powerful arms for three whole beats to flex his muscles, then kneading a dough of bass notes. His eyes glitter. He plays the piano like a drum sometimes—why not?

"Gypsy? Such a dancer?"

"Why you don't hear it straight from your agent? Why it ain't come from headquarters? What you been doing, getting telegrams in the corridor, signed nobody?"

They all laugh. End of that chorus.

"What time is it?" Powerhouse calls. "What the hell place is this? Where is my watch and chain?"

"I hang it on you," whimpers Valentine. "It still there."

There it rides on Powerhouse's great stomach, down where he can never see it.

"Sure did hear some clock striking twelve while ago. Must be midnight."

"It going to be intermission," Powerhouse declares, lifting up his finger with the signet ring.

Powerhouse is a special case. His face and physique demand to be seen; they *are* who he is, in a sense, like Ahab's wooden leg and Daisy's beauty. This changes when your characters are less striking physically. The reader knows what they look like, no need to emphasize it. Only an occasional camera shot is necessary. Think, as you write their dialogue, when it might be useful to the reader to see them gesture, move, or shift their gaze.

Visuals—camera shots—become more useful, and even necessary, in the midst of dialogue when two characters are sexually attracted to each other. Hemingway, advising a young writer, said, "Find what gave you the emotion; what the action was that gave you the excitement. Then write it down making it clear so that the reader will see it too and have the same feeling that you had." In other words, create emotion in the reader by showing him, making him see, what prompts the emotion in your character. (This technique does away with the need for pounding hearts, tingling scalps, gasps, eyes bugging out, and so on; if you can make the reader feel what your character is feeling, she will experience these sensations in her imagination.) When two characters are lovers, or would like to be, show us why. Reinforce the sexual tension of the dialogue with the timely visual.

With this in mind, I made the female protagonist of *The Last Summer*, Claire Malek, a smoker. (Claire's background is blue collar and the year is 1968, so the fact that she smokes doesn't call attention to itself.) The novel is a love story, and I wanted to give Claire a cigarette in certain scenes as a prop. She's sitting at a drugstore counter beside Lane Hillman, the younger man who is falling in love with her:

> "Are you dating anybody?" he said.
>
> She smiled again and opened her purse. He took the matches from her as before and struck one and lifted it to her cigarette. She turned and blew smoke down away from him, and again regarded him with a slow half smile.
>
> "Not at the moment," she said.

A pretty woman on a drugstore stool, turning, tucking her head down near her shoulder to blow smoke, then swinging her gaze around again, struck me as an alluring visual and prelude to her cagey answer to Lane's question. Later they're in bed together:

> She raised herself on her elbow. "Lane, honey there's a few things you have to learn."
>
> "I know," he said.
>
> "Not about sex. About women."
>
> "What?" he said.
>
> She smiled and didn't answer. She leaned in and kissed him, then got up and moved around the room and found her purse. She dug out a cigarette and came back and smoked it sitting up beside him with one leg out straight and the other cocked.
>
> "You're beautiful," he said.

Lane's view of the bare cocked leg preempts conversation for the moment. He's stirred by it, and declares his love. The visual has sent the dialogue in a new direction.

Lee Smith likes to keep her characters in view, especially lovers. In her epistolary novel, *Fair and Tender Ladies*, protagonist Ivy Rowe follows the beekeeper, Honey Breeding—another of Smith's charmers—up the mountain behind her home:

> "Did you go to the war?" I asked.
>
> "I sure did," Honey said. His voice floated back to me over his shoulder. He pulled his shirttail up out of his pants.
>
> "Where did you go?" I asked.
>
> "First I went to Germany," Honey said, "and then I went to France."
>
> We walked on. "I had another older brother that died," I said, "and then a little one that died young. And also I've got another one, Johnny, that I have not seen in a while that plays the piano, and yet one more that is making a preacher."
>
> I couldn't believe I was talking so much, to a perfect stranger!
>
> "See that rock?" I said. "My momma used to come up here and sit on it and cry."
>
> "What did she cry for?" Honey asked.
>
> "Because my daddy was sick, I reckon, and things had not worked out like she thought."
>
> "They never do," Honey said. He walked on before me, up the path. His white shirt flapped in the wind, so white it was dazzling.

Honey is fair and pale-blond, and the snow-white shirt adds to his physical brightness, his glow. He untucks it as he walks, and we see the shirt, and the action, when the wind snatches it. It isn't much—two sentences—but the two brief visuals keep him in sight as he talks. They add a degree of heat to the already-charged dialogue; Ivy is mesmerized, and Smith shows us why.

INTERRUPTING DIALOGUE TO CREATE A NEEDED PAUSE

When there's little reason to inject a visual, the interruption by an action or gesture can give you a needed pause in your dialogue. The pause might be due to uncertainty or nervousness in the speaker, or the speaker might pause knowingly, for dramatic effect, as we often do in real life. Willie Stark, the Machiavellian visionary in Robert Penn Warren's 1946 political classic, *All The King's Men,* is running for governor. Speaking to the crowd at a Sunday barbeque, he finds his political voice and sets his rise to power in motion. He has just realized he's being used by an opponent, Harrison, a revelation that first shocks, then galvanizes Willie Stark. He disregards his written speech and extemporizes, referring to himself in the third person:

> "Those fellows in the striped pants saw the hick and they took him in. They said how MacMurfee was a limber-back and a dead-head and how Joe Harrison was the tool of the city machine, and how they wanted that hick to step in and try to give some honest government. They told him that. But—" Willie stopped, and lifted his right hand, clutching the manuscript to high heaven—"do you know who they were? They were Joe Harrison's hired hands and lickspittles and they wanted to get a hick to run to split MacMurfee's hick vote."

Willie is leveling with the crowd. He recounts the lie that has been told to him, then pauses, gesturing dramatically, letting the lie hang in the air a moment before he demolishes it with the truth. The pause is calculated: Willie is onstage, literally, and he uses it for its effect on his audience, which includes the reader. But a politician is always onstage, in a sense. Willie, now governor, wakes the genteel and venerable Judge Irwin in the middle of the night and helps himself to the judge's whiskey. Jack Burden, Willie's aide and the protagonist of the novel, is narrating:

> When he was back in the leather chair with the fresh load in the glass, he said, "Yeah, Judge, I've heard you say it, but I

wanted to hear you say something else. Are you sure you took it to the Lord in prayer?"

"I have settled the matter in my own mind," the Judge said.

"Well, if I recollect right"—the Boss ruminatively turned the glass in his hands—"back in town" when we had our little talk, you sort of felt my boy Masters was all right."

Willie Stark is a master psychologist and knows how to manipulate people—how to keep them dangling, how to set them up, startle them, catch them off balance. Notice how slowly he's speaking here; his dialogue is slow—Warren doesn't tell us that; the lines *read* slow—and the artful pause slows time itself to a crawl. It's a good visual, using the glass of whiskey as a prop, but the pause here is calculated, by both Willie and the author, more to be heard—an interval of silence—than seen. A good gesture, of course, gets you both.

Don't, however, write gestures that make the dialogue redundant, as happens in real life. Don't have your character nod and then answer a question in the affirmative. (Nods are easy to write. Be selective; really, you seldom need them.) Your character doesn't need to raise a hand, palm out, like a traffic cop, when she tells somebody who's talking too long, "Stop right there." The gesture is implicit, understood, in the command. If you insist on the gesture, cut the line of dialogue. Your character might raise her arms from her sides, palms up, and shrug, but she can't also say, "I haven't the foggiest idea." One or the other, you choose. I usually go with dialogue.

A shrug can be useful, but only when it supplements the line of dialogue and doesn't duplicate it. The indifference or resignation of a shrug can usually be captured in dialogue, making the gesture redundant. But a shrug also might make all the difference. A character, say, facing a firing squad, asked if he has any last words, might shrug and say, "Tell my wife I love her." The shrug colors the declaration with a certain lack of feeling; let's hope they don't report it to the wife.

> **Sighs, like nods and shrugs, are very easy to write—so easy, we sometimes barely notice we're writing them.**

Sighs, like nods and shrugs, are very easy to write—so easy, we sometimes barely notice we're writing them. In editing first novels I find sighs by the dozen, and few of them, if any, give the dialogue any needed help. A shrug is a better visual than a sigh—it is, in its way, an eloquent gesture. But use both sparingly. Sighs were a staple of the heroines of silent movies, and they can have a whiff of melodrama. Fitzgerald's characters are dreamers and likely to sigh from time to time, but not Hemingway's or Faulkner's less sentimental heroes and heroines. A sigh would come off as saccharine and false amid the terse, edgy dialogue of Didion, McCarthy, or William Kennedy. It's impossible to imagine Francis Phelan, the shrewd, life-hardened bum, sighing.

Anne Tyler's characters, on the other hand, are excitable and melodramatic by nature, so of course they sigh. Rebecca Davitch, the middle-aged heroine of *Back When We Were Grownups,* has invited an old flame, Will Allenby, to dinner. The date is bumping along awkwardly. The phone rings, rings again:

> "You certainly get a lot of calls," Will told her.
>
> "Yes," she said. She sighed. "Won't you have more chicken?"

The evening is disappointing and wearying Rebecca, but she's too full of conflicting emotions, too naturally forgiving, to indicate this in words, as a Didion character could not help doing. Instead of the sly or mordant ironic remark, Rebecca sighs.

Like exclamation points, sighs and their frequency are up to you, and your characters. I try to avoid them. You don't have to, but keep the frequency to a minimum. They're easy to write, as I've said—often too easy.

INTERRUPTING DIALOGUE TO STOP TIME

Very often, a single speech of even a few words turns the story. Such lines are revelatory, often startling, sometimes shocking, and, like surprises in real life, they take a moment to sink in. When this happens, you, the writer, have to stop time. Beginning writers tend to overlook this necessity. A character in the beginner's novel might break some surprising news to his wife, and the scene might go like this:

> "I wasn't at the Elks meeting last night," Larry said.
> "Oh? And just where were you, if I might ask?"
> "I was with Tiffany."
> "God," Susan said, "how could you?"

There isn't anything wrong with this dialogue, in itself. What *is* wrong, assuming Larry is the uxorious type, is Susan's immediate response. Susan needs a moment to absorb this new development, and so does the reader. Arrest the moment. Freeze it. A pause, and then the story resumes, taking a new direction.

In Elmore Leonard's darkly comic short story, *When the Women Come Out to Dance,* Ginger Mahmood, an ex-stripper married to a Pakistani plastic surgeon in south Florida, hires a shady Columbian maid named Lourdes. Lourdes, Ginger happens to know, recently had her abusive husband, a man named Zimmer, murdered. (Lourdes has useful friends who are also recent arrivals from Columbia.) Ginger would like to get rid of her own creepy husband, but there was a prenuptial agreement stipulating that she gets nothing if she divorces him. She explains this, in a veiled way, to Lourdes, sitting on the poolside patio. Leonard is writing Lourdes' point of view:

> Lourdes believed the woman was very close to telling her what she was thinking about. Still, it was not something easy to talk about with another person, even for a woman who danced naked. Lourdes decided this evening to help her.
>
> She said, "How would you feel if a load of concrete fell on your husband?"

Then wondered, sitting in the silence, not looking at the woman, if she had spoken too soon.

The redheaded woman said, "The way it happened to Mr. Zimmer? How did you feel?"

"I accepted it," Lourdes said, "with a feeling of relief, knowing I wouldn't be beaten no more."

Lourdes' question is an offer to have Ginger's husband murdered, and Leonard arrests the moment while the news sinks in. Ginger has no moral objection to the idea, but even so, she needs that moment to digest it. You *have* to create a pause after a line like this; if there were no interval here, Lourdes' proposal would be cheated of the attention it deserves. *How would you feel if a load of concrete fell on your husband?* Give a line like that—it's a beauty—some time. Give it some room.

Robert Penn Warren arrests a different kind of moment, a deeply troubling discovery by Jack Burden, in *All The King's Men*. Jack was in love with his neighbor, Anne Stanton, in his youth, and may still be. The very proper Anne has been referring to Willie Stark disdainfully as "that man," and Jack strikes back at her in defense of his boss:

"You take the same snobbish attitude all the rest take. You're like the rest."

"All right," she said, still not looking at me. "I'm snobbish. I'm so snobbish I had lunch with him last week."

Well, if grandfather's clock in the corner hadn't been stopped already, that would have stopped it. It stopped me. I heard the flame hum on the logs, gnawing in. Then the hum stopped and there wasn't anything.

Then I said, "For Christ's sake." And the absorbent silence sucked up the words like blotting paper.

"All right," she said, "for Christ's sake."

"My, my," I said, "but the picture of the daughter of Governor Stanton at lunch with Governor Stark would certainly throw the society editor of the Chronicle into a tizzy. Your frock, my dear—what frock did you wear? And flowers? Did you drink champagne cocktails?"

The timing in this interchange is perfect. Jack, annoyed by Anne's superior-seeming attitude toward the populist governor, is blindsided by the news that she has sat down to lunch with him. Jack senses immediately what this might presage, and the presentiment prompts a rush of alarm and jealousy. Warren freezes time almost literally with his allusion to the stopped clock, then has us listen to the hearth fire while Jack struggles with this new circumstance. Anne Stanton is highly principled, and Jack has always idealized her both as a woman and a paragon of integrity. That she would do business over lunch with Willie Stark shakes Jack's world. The story turns here, and Warren arrests the moment, bringing it into sharp focus.

Jack finds his voice, finally, but it takes one more line, and a defiant reply from Anne, for him to recover enough to couch his displeasure in mockery. Once he does, Warren gets out of the way and lets the colloquy move briskly—and heatedly—to its end.

The plot of *Seen the Glory* turns radically with a line of dialogue on the field at Gettysburg, the night before Pickett's Charge. Thomas Chandler presses his older brother Luke to tell him the name of the girl he loved, and slept with, back home on Martha's Vineyard:

> Luke, blanket-draped and hugging his knees, drew a deep breath.
> "Rose," he said.
> "Rose?"
> "Yeah."
> "Not our Rose," Thomas said.
> Luke did not look at him. He nodded.

> "Rose Miranda?" Thomas said.
>
> "Yes."
>
> "You liar."
>
> Luke didn't answer.
>
> "You Goddamn liar."

Thomas is secretly in love with Rose, the Chandlers' slightly older—and beautiful—housekeeper, and Luke's affair with her, of which Thomas had no inkling, staggers and enrages him—when it finally sinks in. The dialogue stalls here, like a stuck record. Thomas keeps asking the same question and getting the same answer; he's hoping for a different answer, a clarification or retraction that will erase this sudden blow to the heart. It's a vain hope, as he knows deep down, and when it is gone—when the truth has sunk in—he lashes out at his brother, and time begins moving again.

McCarthy, in *All the Pretty Horses*, arrests a fateful moment, not after, but *before* John Grady Cole tells the lie that will turn the story in the worst possible way for him. The proprietor, the *hacendado,* of the ranch in Mexico where John Grady and Rawlins are now working, is querying John Grady with the idea of promoting him. They are drinking coffee and smoking expensive cigarettes in the big dining room. Four cats—McCarthy is setting something up—are sitting on the windowsill all in a row, "like cutout cats all leaning slightly aslant." The *hacendado* tests John Grady's knowledge of horses, and then:

> You are from Christoval?
>
> San Angelo. Or just outside of San Angelo.
>
> The hacendado studied him. Do you know a book called *The Horse of America*, by Wallace?
>
> Yessir. I've read it front to back.
>
> The hacendado leaned back in the chair. One of the cats rose and stretched.
>
> You rode here from Texas.

Yessir.

You and your friend.

Yessir.

Just the two of you?

John Grady looked at the table. The paper cat stepped thin and slant among the shapes of cats thereon. He looked up again. Yessir, he said. Just me and him.

The hacendado nodded and stubbed out his cigarette and pushed back his chair. Come, he said, I will show you some horses.

• • •

But, as the reader well knows, there was a third traveler, an enigmatic boy, possibly a criminal, who was running from a Mexican posse when John Grady and Rawlins last saw him. John Grady Cole is no liar—in two novels he tells only this one—and McCarthy arrests the moment while John Grady deliberates telling it. There's terrific drama here; we know what John Grady is thinking, and we know that his answer will be fraught with consequences, either way. The moment of stopped time brings his dilemma, and his difficulty in dealing with it, into bold focus. It's a turning point, and the reader doesn't forget it.

• • •

You can arrest a moment, briefly, by having a character look at another between lines of dialogue. A caution, though: you can't use "looked at" often or indiscriminately. Usually when a character is speaking, we assume she's looking at the person, or persons, she's addressing. No need to tell us; we see it that way unless you tell us otherwise—she's looking off into the distance, say, or looking down at her lap. We assume, also, that the person being spoken to is looking at *her.*

But when you spell it out, "Ed looked at Julia," you're telling the reader that more is going on than the natural way we look at each other when speaking. "Ed looked at Julia": it's a special look, quick or sudden, a look of new interest, or maybe of annoyance, maybe of appeal. Be wary of describing the look—"he looked imploringly," "he looked anxiously," "he looked longingly." The nature of the look should be evident in what elicits it, for one thing. For another, an adverb limits it, preempting the reader's imagination. "Ed looked at Julia": there might be longing *and* anxiety, and more, in the look. Let the reader imagine the look—it will be more vivid and nuanced than your adverb can make it.

No one word could nail the look which Inez Victor, the protagonist of Didion's ironically titled novel, *Democracy,* gives her husband's political aide, Billy Dillon, in the corridor of the hospital where Inez's sister is on life support. A young doctor is being evasive about the sister's condition:

> "It's not necessarily an either or situation, Mrs. Victor."
> "Life and death? Are not necessarily either-or?"
> "Inez," Billy Dillon said.
> "I want to get this straight. Is that what he's saying?"
> "I'm saying there's a certain gray area, which may or may not be—"
> Inez looked at Billy Dillon.
> "He's saying she won't make it," Billy Dillon said.

The three characters here are looking at each other as they talk; people always do. But Inez's patience runs out, she wants the truth, and her look at Billy is a *particular* look, which the imagination sees as inquiring, irritable, insistent. It creates a pause and elicits Billy Dillon's blunt assertion of the truth.

In Howard Frank Mosher's comic and charming baseball novel, *Waiting for Teddy Williams*—set, as all of Mosher's fiction is, in the Northeast Kingdom of Vermont—a stranger named Teddy begins showing up in town to school the boy, Kinneson, in the finer points of his beloved game of baseball:

> One morning a brand-new pair of size-eight spikes appeared on the mound. Inside each shoe was a new sweat sock. E.A. sat on the Packard seat to put them on.

"Teach me something new today," he wheedled

"All right," Teddy said. "Wear them socks inside out the first few times."

E.A. looked at him.

"Cuts down on the blisters," Teddy explained.

Looked at him: it's a puzzled look, a look of sudden interest. They've *been* looking at each other, but this look is different.

Later in *Democracy*, Inez and Harry Victor are having dinner in a restaurant with their children, Adlai and Jessie. Adlai says he wants to write an op ed piece for the *New York Times*. Don't miss the tension here:

"It's something we've been tossing back and forth in Cambridge."

"Interesting," Harry Victor said. "Let me vet it. What do you think, Jess?"

"I think he shouldn't say 'Cambridge,'" Jessie said.

"Possibly you were nodding out when I went up there," Adlai said, "but Cambridge happens to be where I went to school."

"Maybe so," Jessie said, "but you don't happen to go to Harvard."

"OK guys. You both fouled." Harry Victor turned to Adlai. "I could vet somebody at the Times. If you're serious."

"Turned to" is like "looked at." It signifies something more than the natural swing of attention from one person to another. When Harry Victor says, "What do you think, Jess?" we see him turning to her, without Didion's telling us that he does. He's speaking to her. He's looking at her. He *had* to have turned to her. A few lines down, "Harry turned to Adlai," and the turning this time is pointed—he's speaking past Jessie, excluding her. He's giving Adlai his full attention.

> **"Looked at" and "turned to" are telling actions, but only if you save them for telling moments.**

"Looked at" and "turned to" are telling actions, but only if you save them for telling moments. Spend wisely, and you'll get value every time.

• • •

In the speech that ignites both the barbecue crowd and his political career in *All The King's Men*, Willie Stark pauses multiple times, for effect. Early on, "Willie paused, and blinked around at the crowd. And again: "He paused, steadied himself by the table, and took a deep breath while the sweat dripped." Still later, "He paused and wiped the sweat off his face with his left hand, a flat scouring motion."

Each time, Warren tells us that Willie pauses—stops speaking, that is—then writes the action that occurs during the pause. Once, though, the word "paused" isn't used:

> "There!" Willie roared. "There!" And he waved his right hand, the hand clutching the manuscript of his speech. "There is the Judas Iscariot, the lickspittle, the nose-wiper!"

What's the difference between the first three pauses and this one? Suppose Warren hadn't used "paused" and written only the action, as he does here?

> Willie blinked around at the crowd again.
> He steadied himself by the table, and took a deep breath while the sweat dripped.
> He wiped the sweat off his face with his left hand, a flat scouring motion.

Is there a difference? Does the writer need to tell the reader that a character pauses? *All The King's Men* won the Pulitzer Prize, and Robert Penn Warren was America's first poet laureate, so no one's going to quibble with his word choices or narrative technique. Many writers use "paused" regularly.

I'm a dissenter. Create your pauses. The action *is* the pause. *Alvin paused and looked out at the garbage truck. Alvin looked out at the garbage truck*. What's the difference? We know Alvin has stopped talking; that's what a close quote means. In the pause, he looks out at the garbage truck.

In *Plainsong*, Maggie Jones is talking to the pregnant teenager, Victoria Robideaux, at her kitchen table asking Victoria about the father of her child:

> He was nice to me. He would tell me things.
> Would he?
> Yes. He told me things.
> Like what for instance?
> Like once he said I had beautiful eyes. He said my eyes were like black diamonds lit up on a starry night.
> They are, honey.
> But nobody ever told me.
> No, Maggie said. They never do. She looked out through the doorway into the other room. She lifted her teacup and drank from it and set it down. Go on, she said. Do you want to tell the rest?

Maggie's actions comprise the pause; Haruf never uses the word. It's a longish pause; Haruf devotes three verbs to Maggie's sip of tea, drawing the action out, lengthening the pause. Maggie is thinking about what she has just said, *They never do,* and is struck suddenly by something she and the girl have in common, disappointment in a man or men. The pause tells us this. Maggie Jones has known disappointment. Many writers use "paused," and you can, too. Take it a case at a time, and consider whether the action or actions create the pause effectively, by themselves. You might decide, as I did, that they do, every time.

6

TELLING STORY THROUGH DIALOGUE

A friend called and said he'd written a novel and asked if I would edit it. It consisted largely of dialogue, he said, and wondered if that would be a problem. "There's no such thing as too much dialogue," I said.

I had spoken too soon. The novel was set up this way: the protagonist, a middle-aged woman who has led a rich life both professionally and amorously, is lunching with a former beau in a New York delicatessen. The old boyfriend asks questions, and the questions elicit stories. The stories were pretty good, or had the potential to be: love affairs gone hilariously awry, sexism triumphantly overturned in the workplace. The trouble was the narrative voice. The stories were being told in a sly, chatty, zestful way that made fairly good dialogue but lacked the range, elasticity, and vocabulary for the long haul of sustained dramatic narrative. The narrative sounded like what it was: a woman regaling a close friend in a restaurant. The stories came tumbling out, lively but abbreviated, like a highlights film.

You're leaving too much out, I told my friend. If Sophie's going to tell her own story in the form of dialogue with a friend, I said, you've got to give her a stronger narrative voice. A change of venue might help, I said—something less public, with more ambiance: a place conducive to reflection and reminiscence.

> **The device of the storyteller as narrator goes back to *The Canterbury Tales* and involves a tacit understanding between writer and reader.**

The device of the storyteller as narrator goes back to *The Canterbury Tales* and involves a tacit understanding between writer and reader. Charles Marlow is Joseph Conrad's storyteller in his great novellas, *Heart of Darkness, Chance,* and *Youth,* and for most of his classic novel, *Lord Jim*.

THE FIRST PERSON NARRATIVE OF CONRAD'S CHARLEY MARLOW

Heart of Darkness, at one level, takes place at nightfall on the deck of the yawl *Nellie*, at anchor on the Thames, where her crew is lying around waiting for the tide to change. Conrad sets the scene in his emotive and inimitable way—the sun going down, sky and water darkening, some "lazy" words among the men. By and by Marlow begins to talk:

"I was thinking of very old times, when the Romans first came here, nineteen hundred years ago—the other day. Light came out of this river since—you say knights? Yes; but it is like a running blaze on a plain, like a flash of lightning in the clouds. We live in the flicker—may it last as long as the old earth keeps rolling! But darkness was here yesterday."

Marlow goes on, gradually shaping the tale of his voyage, as ship's captain, deep into the Belgian Congo—that literal and metaphorical heart of darkness. Marlow's narrative, strictly speaking, is dialogue; it is set off by quotation marks throughout, and is interrupted from time to time by a remark by one of his listeners, and, once, by Marlow relighting his pipe, during which we get a vivid look at him in the flare of the match. It's dialogue, but dialogue that's as rich, coherent, and well-ordered as any first-person narrative:

> "And in the hush that had fallen suddenly upon the whole sorrowful
> land, the immense wilderness, the colossal body of the fecund and
> mysterious life seemed to look at her, pensive, as though it had been
> looking at the image of its own tenebrous and passionate soul."

Nobody talks like this, but so what? We settle on the deck of the
yawl, in the dying light, glad to be there, and to listen.

Conrad sets the stage for Marlow somewhat differently in *Lord
Jim*. We're at a dinner gathering thirty pages in, on a "verandah draped
in motionless foliage and crowned with flowers," when Charley
Marlow takes up the narrative, by request:

> ". . . Charley, my dear chap, your dinner was extremely good,
> and in consequence these men here look upon a quiet game of
> rubber as a tumultuous occupation. They wallow in your good
> chairs and think, 'Hang exertion. Let that Marlow talk.'"

Marlow does, for three hundred seventy pages: nearly four
hundred pages of uninterrupted dialogue.

THE HENRY WIGGEN NOVELS: A STORYTELLER'S DIALOGUE WITH A DIFFERENCE

Mark Harris, who died in 2007, was best known for his four novels
about Henry Wiggen, memoirist and star left-handed pitcher for the
big-league New York Mammoths. Henry is shrewd, flippant, and
indifferently educated, and his narrative voice, colloquial and colorful,
has been compared to Huckleberry Finn's. Harris's most acclaimed
novel—he wrote thirteen in all—was the third in the Henry Wiggen
series, *Bang the Drum Slowly*, which begins:

> Me and Holly were laying around in bed around 10 A.M. on a
> Wednesday morning when the call come. I was slow answering

it, thinking first of a comical thing to say, though I suppose it long since stopped handing anybody a laugh except me. I don't know. I laugh at a lot of things nobody ever laughs at except her.

Henry's own dialogue, like Huck Finn's, is the same as his narrative voice. Well, of course: he talks to people the same way he talks to the reader. But a curious thing happens when *other* people speak in the Henry Wiggen novels: they talk just like Henry. Same diction, same quirky style and voice, same vocabulary. There are idiosyncrasies galore in the dialogue. In this scene from *Bang the Drum Slowly*, Henry "Author" Wiggen is haggling over his contract with the owners of the Mammoths in a Florida hotel room:

> I said, "Leave us not waste time talking contract unless you are willing to talk contract. I was taught in school where slavery went out when Lincoln was shot."
>
> "I know," said Old Man Moors, "for you wrote it across the top of your contract."
>
> "Not across my contract," I said. "Maybe across the contract of a turnstile turner."
>
> "Author," said Patricia, "leave us all calm down." She was very beautiful that night, and I said so, and she thanked me. Her nose was quite sunburned. "You are looking over your weight," she said. "It will no doubt take you many weeks to get in shape."
>
> "He looks 10 pounds over his weight at least," said Bradley Lord.
>
> "Mr. Bradley Lord," said I, whipping out my loose cash. "I have $200 here which says I am no more than 2 and 3/8 pounds over my weight if you would care to go and fetch the bathroom scale."
>
> "What do you consider your absolute minimum figure?" said Mr. Moors.
>
> "19,000," I said.
>
> "In that case," said he, "we can simply never do business, and I suppose I must be put to the trouble of scouring up another left-hand pitcher."

"That should not be hard," said I, "for I seen several promising boys out there this afternoon. Any one of them will win 4 or 5 games if God drops everything else."

"In this book," writes Twain in an 'Explanation' at the front of *Huckleberry Finn,* "a number of dialects are used, to wit: the Missouri Negro dialect; the extremest form of the backwoods Southwestern dialect; the ordinary 'Pike County' dialect; and four modified varieties of this last." In other words, the dialogue in the novel is genuine—we hear what Huck hears.

"Stand by you!" Mary Jane Wilks tells Huck. "Indeed I will. They sha'nt touch a hair of your head." Mary Jane's voice is her own. She speaks past Huck, to us. This has been the convention in first-person narratives going back to Swift and Dafoe.

But Mark Harris, as Henry Wiggen, puts his own stamp on his characters' dialogue. The conceit is that the novels are memoirs; it is after publication of the first in the series, *The Southpaw,* that Henry's team-mates begin calling him "Author." The dialogue, the reader understands, is not what Henry hears. It is reconstructed, *written* by Henry Wiggen. We know that Patricia Moors didn't say, "Leave us all calm down," and the conjunction in her father's "I know, for you wrote it across the top of your contract" gives the line a comical and implausible formality. There are no contractions in the dialogue—*unless you are willing, that should not be hard*—and we understand that Henry hasn't been schooled in their use.

The result speaks for itself and is proof of Mark Harris's virtuosity. The dialogue in his Henry Wiggen novels, so novel and eccentric, is like all good dialogue in one necessary way—it's an extrapolation, a creative improvement over the real thing. It has a tone and melody of its own. The Henry Wiggen novels on one level are comic—even *Bang the Drum Slowly,* in which Henry's teammate and friend, Bruce Pearson, is dying of Hodgkin's Lymphoma—and Harris's dialogue is some of the funniest ever written. It is funny, in part, because its syntax and idioms are Henry's own. The dialogue doesn't sound real, but that's beside the point; Harris has made a different arrangement with the reader.

Damon Runyon made the same arrangement in his diverting short stories of Broadway. Some vintage Runyon dialogue from *Breach of Promise*:

> Harry the Horse pounds me on the back to keep me from choking, and while he pounds so hard that he almost caves in my spine, I consider it a most courteous action, and when I am able to talk again, I say to him as follows:
>
> "Well, Harry," I say, "it is a privilege and a pleasure to see you again, and I hope and trust you will all join me in some cold borscht, which you will find very nice, indeed."
>
> "No," Harry says, "we do not care for any cold borscht. We are looking for Judge Goldfobber. Do you see Judge Goldfobber round and about lately?"
>
> Well, the idea of Harry the Horse and Spanish John and Little Isadore looking for Judge Goldfobber sounds somewhat alarming to me, and I figure maybe the job Judge Goldfobber gives them turns out bad and they wish to take Judge Goldfobber apart, but the next minute Harry says to me like this:
>
> "By the way," he says, "we wish to thank you for the job of work you throw our way. Maybe some day we will be able to do as much for you. It is a most interesting job," Harry says, "and while you are snuffing your cold borscht I will give you the details, so you will understand why we wish to see Judge Goldfobber."

Runyon's characters are gamblers, loan sharks, small-time gangsters, waitresses, club dancers, and street missionaries, and they don't talk like this any more than Patricia Moors says, "Leave us all calm down." Runyon was a great humorist, and his dialogue, like Mark Harris's, is relentlessly comic. It reads as if his hustlers and hangers-on were affecting a high-bred gentility in their speech, and failing ludicrously.

Oddly, Jo Swerling and Abe Burrows, writing the book for the Runyon-inspired musical, *Guys and Dolls,* took the dialogue straight from Runyon's two stories, *Blood Pressure* and *The Idyll of Miss Sarah Brown,* preserving its orotund constructions and omission of contractions. At the end of Act I, the natty and virile gambler, Sky Masterson, finds the beautiful Sarah Brown at work in the Save-a-Soul Mission, and the conversation quickly turns personal:

> Sky: "It is nice to know, Miss Sarah, that somewhere there is a guy who will appeal to you. I wonder what this guy will be like."
> Sarah: "He will not be a gambler."
> Sky: "I am not interested in what he will not be. I am interested in what he will be."

The absence of contractions gives the dialogue, here and throughout the show, an artificial and implausible dignity, and I've sometimes wondered why Swerling and Burrows made this choice. Mark Harris made the same choice when he wrote the screenplay for the 1973 movie version of *Bang the Drum Slowly*. In Harris's script the dialogue is generally cleansed of contractions, as it is in his novel. Even the Georgia hayseed, Bruce Pearson, played by Robert De Niro, speaks without shortening "was not," "will not," "have not," and so on. The tough-talking manager of the Mammoths, Dutch Schnell, played by Vincent Gardenia, doesn't use contractions. There 's an odd similarity between the baseball movie and the Broadway musical.

Guys and Dolls is one of Broadway's most endearing musicals, and *Bang the Drum Slowly* is an esteemed film that retains its charm and poignancy after more than forty years. The dialogue works in both, obviously, as it does in Runyon's stories and Harris's Henry Wiggen novels: we enjoy it, simply, for what it is.

MULTIPLE STORYTELLERS

Most of Faulkner's brooding and brilliant novel, *Absalom, Absalom!* is dialogue in the way that *Heart of Darkness* and *Lord Jim* are, with the difference that Faulkner uses three storytellers as narrators: the old

woman, Rosa Coldfield, young Quentin Compson, and—briefly—
Quentin's father. The dialogue isn't plausible any more than Charles
Marlow's is. Quentin, in his room at Harvard, is talking to Shreve, his
roommate:

> "And he not calling it retribution, no sins of the father come
> home to roost; not even calling it luck, but just a mistake: that
> mistake which he could not discover himself and which he came
> to Grandfather, not to excuse, but just to review the facts for an
> impartial (and Grandfather said he believed, a legally trained)
> mind to examine and find and point out to him."

Quentin is both listener—to his father, to Rosa—and storyteller,
to Shreve in their cold room late at night. The settings are powerfully
evoked, and Faulkner never lets us forget where we are as we listen in.
Rosa Coldfield has invited Quentin into her "office," with its "dim coffin-
smelling gloom sweet and over-sweet with the twice-bloomed wistaria
against the outer wall," where he will sit through the long September
afternoon while the old woman opens the story of the implacable Henry
Sutpen and his offspring. She is leading up to a request, which Quentin
will agree to, and which will touch off the novel's fierce climax.

Quentin listens in silence to Rosa, but his Harvard roommate
Shreve is nowhere near as passive, and his interjections, which are
often lengthy, are a counterpoint to Quentin's narrative, and a crucial
influence on the telling. Shreve is Canadian and has a cynical view
of the American South; Quentin, troubled and defensive, is carrying
on a kind of argument with his friend, trying to explain and justify
the land of his forebears, with its tormented and violent history. In
truth, as the reader knows, Quentin is trying to convince himself, as
well as Shreve.

It all adds up to one of the greatest of American novels,
and no discussion of dialogue can ignore its unusual narrative

strategy. Faulkner's understanding with the reader, like Conrad's, is acceptance—Samuel Taylor Coleridge's "suspension of disbelief." Rosa is talking to Quentin, Quentin to Shreve. The dialogue isn't real . . . but it is. That's the deal. Enjoy it

PLAUSIBLE DIALOGUE AS NARRATIVE: THE ORDINARY STORYTELLER

Conrad, in his Marlow novels, and Faulkner in *Absalom, Absalom!* erased the distinction between first-person narrator and a storyteller within the novel, a rare strategy in fiction. The Marlow novels and *Absalom, Absalom!* are written in the third person, strictly speaking, but Conrad speaks to the reader directly, *as* Marlow, and Faulkner as Quentin and Rosa Coldfield. Rosa's story to Quentin, and Quentin's to Shreve, could as easily have been presented as conventional first-person narratives. There's no law against multiple first-person narratives in a novel; Lee Smith uses them all the time, handing the narrative off from character to character down through two and three generations. Keep the option in mind.

What about the ordinary storyteller? Marlow's narrative, as he lolls on the deck of the yawl, carries an entire novel, but Marlow is no ordinary storyteller, as we've seen. When do you turn the narrative over to an ordinary storyteller, and for how long?

It depends on the story—its importance, and who is in it. The reader isn't going to suspend disbelief with regard to the storyteller's voice and diction, as we do with Marlow and Quentin, so the story has to be told in the character's speaking voice. This means dialogue, with its quirks, subjectivity, and colloquialisms. The story will be compact, as all dialogue must be. It will be short on detail.

In John Sayles's 1977 novel about 1960s radicalism, *Union Dues*, the West Virginia coal miner Hunter McNatt is giving a history lesson to fellow conspirators at a clandestine union meeting:

"One night some of these agents killed a union organizer, blasted him right off'n his front porch from their car while Luther and the other folks that lived by him looked on. They brought it to the Sheriff, said they could recognize faces and names and all, but Sheriff said no, it was too dark to see. Wouldn't make an arrest. Well, people expected as much, so Luther and some of the other fellas who was tryin to bring the union in, they took it on themselves. Laid out all night with their rifles, waitin for a couple of the agents to come by this tavern used to be up the hill a piece from here. Eye for an eye they figured.

"Only there was spies in amongst them. The Sheriff and the agents got word and come down out of the pines around midnight, catching these miners from behind. Luther, he took one in the meat of the shoulder and one half-tored his buttock off . . ."

Hunter McNatt's narrative voice here is eloquent in a folksy way, and it's easy to imagine it carrying an entire novel. But this is dialogue, and Hunter puts a story of murder, betrayal, and a shootout in a nutshell, as anyone would, telling it orally. In two sentences Hunter recounts the miners' visit to the sheriff, their informing him that one of their own has been murdered and the sheriff's refusal to do anything about it: Sayles, if he'd taken over the narrative and written a flashback, could have spun this out into a tense and dramatic confrontation. Imagine the sheriff on the porch, the men in the dark just below him; imagine the taut dialogue. Sayles then could have put us on the hillside in the dark and written the eruption of gunfire, the ambush, men being hit, bullets singing in the air.

Why didn't he?

For one thing, he didn't want to leave the back room of the darkened bar, where the union meeting is being held. He wanted to keep us at the meeting, instead of transporting us back in time to the sheriff's house, and to the pine woods and the shooting. Hunter's story is an interruption of the business at hand—the union leader,

Luther, has been denigrated as a sellout, and Hunter feels compelled to give some perspective to the younger men in the room—and Sayles wants to keep the interruption brief. And there is this: Luther is a minor character, and a blow-by-blow account of the events Hunter describes would bring him, Luther, too far into the foreground. It would put too much focus on him.

You make this choice every time a character begins to tell a story: let the character tell it, or take over yourself. In a novel by a student of mine, the male and female protagonists, husband and wife, first met in a fashionable bar in Paris, where a pianist was playing Cole Porter songs. It was love at first sight. Years later the wife describes the meeting to a female friend over drinks at a rooftop bar in Manhattan—the reader's only witness to the event.

I urged the author—begged her—to write the scene in the Parisian bar in her own narrative voice, as a flashback. I said it needed a full telling, from moment to moment: action dialogue, ambiance, the strains of "Let's Fall In Love" and "Night and Day." The event was too important to be left to Julia over cocktails. The reader needed to be there, not hear it secondhand.

Screenplay writers make the choice all the time, with the same considerations as the novelist. A flashback clears the screen and resets it, transposing us to another place and time. A new narrative takes us over; for the time being, we've left the context—the trigger of the flashback, the storyteller, if there is one—behind. The question, always, is simple: how important is the story?

Claire Malek, my female protagonist in *The Last Summer*, has left Washington, D.C., and her job as secretary to a United States senator, in a hurry. It's clear to the reader that she's suffered a betrayal of some sort, but Claire refuses to talk about it, even to her fifteen-year-old daughter. Nearly halfway into the novel, Lane Hillman, in love with Claire by now, takes her to the theater and then to a piano bar. The play was a romantic musical, the pianist is playing Johnny Mathis, and Claire's mood turns wistful and reflective. Lane asks her what

happened in Washington. She's trying, with less and less success, to
deflect his youthful and gentlemanly advances:

> "Tell me what happened," he said.
> *Then he'll stop. Then this will be over and I can live a normal*
> *life again and find someone who's right for me.*
> "Ask the waitress for another round," she said.

There's a text break here, and the flashback begins in a car on a
highway outside of Washington. Midnight, Claire in the passenger
seat, her boss driving. It is very dark. He's speeding. If the novel were a
movie, the flashback would occur the same way. No screenplay writer
would let Claire tell the story herself; it was a wrenching turning
point in her life, and she's the female protagonist, so we need the tale
in full. The film audience would get the story as Claire experienced
it, not as she would tell it. So does the reader in my novel.

The flashback runs to sixteen pages. Text break, and:

> Now they sat in the dark in the vinyl-smelling Chevy, looking
> out at the bay. They could hear the waves, slow and sibilant, on
> the shore below. The misted moon spread a dull pewter sheen
> on the water.
> "I wanted to go see Tyrone Moore's mother," Claire said. "I
> called the state police and got the name of the funeral home. The
> funeral home gave me the address. It was in a real bad section.
> "I was afraid to go there alone, even in the daytime. I asked
> Mark to go with me. 'One last favor,' I said, 'and then we're even.' I
> said if he came with me I'd tell Mrs. Moore I was driving. 'Which you
> were,' Mark said. Then he said he was busy and hung up on me.
> "I didn't know who else to ask. I wasn't going to take a girl
> into that neighborhood. I tried a couple guys I knew who weren't
> on Bob's staff. I tried a guy I'd dated for a while. I was leaving in a

few days, and all of them were afraid or busy or just didn't want to bother. So I never went."

Lane and Claire have had a second drink and left the bar by the time she gets to the end of her story: the reader knows she's been talking for a long time. (It was still *told* to Lane, not *seen* by him; the reader was there, Lane was not, but the distinction disappears; it is a given that Lane and the reader are equally affected—another tacit understanding with the reader.) Claire finishes the account herself, covering several days in three short paragraphs—a brief coda, which Claire can articulate, as storyteller, as well as I could, and which returns the reader not just to Cape Cod on a summer night, but to a close shot of Claire—all the way back to the present.

TAKING EXPOSITION OUT OF DIALOGUE

The storyteller is talking to somebody in your novel, as well as to the reader. The listener, or listeners, might know more than the reader does; be aware of this, and don't let your storyteller tell other characters things they already know in order to impart the information to your reader. You're forcing your dialogue when you do this. We don't do this in real life, and when you do it in fiction it stands out like the proverbial sore thumb. This is known as "exposition through dialogue." Avoid it.

"Dad left for work at seven," Jimmy tells his sister, Greta, let's say, on page one. It's a bad line, because work is where Dad goes every morning, and Greta knows it.

"Dad left for the bank at seven," Jimmy says, another bad line, written with the idea of letting the reader know that Dad is a banker. Find another way. Greta knows Dad's a banker, and Jimmy knows she knows it.

What Jimmy is probably going to say—he would in my novel—is, "Dad left at seven."

Then how do you inform the reader that Dad is a banker? There are two ways. Drop in a line of simple exposition—early, but not too early:

> "Dad left at seven," Jimmy said.
> "Why so early?" Greta said.
> "I think he's seeing someone," Jimmy said.
> Charles Kaufman was president of the Queen's County Savings Bank, down at the foot of Main Street by the village green. He was president of Rotary and chairman of the hospital's board of directors.
> "No way," Greta said.

Withhold Charles's position at least until Jimmy's second line, which, you can reasonably hope, will gain the reader's full attention and curiosity. *Who is this guy who may be having an affair?* Charles Kaufman's job and position in the community are suddenly interesting.

Or, instead of an early expository sentence or two, you can let the dialogue do the revealing, but in a plausible way:

> "I think he's seeing someone," Jimmy said.
> "No way," Greta said.
> "I was at the bank yesterday, and I saw this hot young redhead go into his office. She was in there a long time."
> "So what?"
> "Greta, he's the frigging president. What's he doing talking to a twenty-year-old for an hour?"

Fiction is revelation, and timing is everything.

Disclosure doesn't have to come immediately, or all at once. I tell students constantly: the reader will wait. It's okay, in fact, to keep him wondering for a while. Fiction is revelation, and timing is everything. Make sure your characters are speaking to each other, not to the reader. There are other ways besides forced dialogue, and there's plenty of time to reveal that your character is a deep-sea diver or an economics professor at Berkeley.

· · ·

Occasionally, and you want to avoid it when you can, a character must tell a story that the reader already knows, has been witness to. The cardinal requirement of dialogue is unpredictability, some

> **The cardinal requirement of dialogue is unpredictability.**

element of discovery or surprise, and your character might tell the familiar story in a way so colorful and subjective that it sheds new light on the story itself, or on the character telling it. He might exaggerate, if that's in character, or leave something out, or invent something that didn't happen, and there's surprise in that, of course.

If the storyteller is a straight talker, set his dialogue aside and boil the story down for him. For John Grady Cole it's a question of *what* he tells Magdalena, not *how*, in their final liaison in *All the Pretty Horses*:

> He told her about Blevins and about the prison Castelar and he told her about what happened to Rawlins and finally he told her about the cuchillero who had fallen dead in his arms with his knife broken off in his heart. He told her everything.

We know all of this. We were there. We don't need to hear the story again, so McCarthy compacts it into two sentences, which let us know that he has held nothing back.

INDIRECT DISCOURSE

You might want to pare a story down, but not strip it of all color and nuance. Indirect discourse is a compromise, halfway between dialogue and exposition.

· · ·

Atticus Finch won't talk to Jem and Scout about his hostile encounter with Bob Ewell after the trial of Tom Robinson, but their loquacious neighbor will:

According to Miss Stephanie Crawford, however, Atticus was leaving the post office when Mr. Ewell approached him, cursed him, spat on him, and threatened to kill him . . . Miss Stephanie said Atticus didn't bat an eye, just took out his handkerchief and wiped his face and stood there and let Mr. Ewell call him names wild horses could not bring her to repeat. Mr. Ewell was a veteran of an obscure war; that plus Atticus's peaceful reaction probably prompted him to inquire, "Too proud to fight, you nigger-lovin bastard?" Miss Stephanie said Atticus said, "No, too old," put his hands in his pockets and strolled on. Miss Stephanie said you had to hand it to Atticus Finch, he could be right dry sometimes.

Harper Lee doesn't want Scout, or us, to see the menace in this incident—which is a prelude to Bob Ewell's attack on Jem and Scout—until later, in retrospect. The confrontation would have frightened Scout had she seen it, but she gets it second-hand from Miss Stephanie, who seems to have missed its latent viciousness. Scout—Lee—could as easily have given us Miss Stephanie's account word for word, as dialogue, but Lee uses indirect discourse here to diminish the impact of a sinister event. If Scout had quoted Miss Stephanie instead of paraphrasing her, we would likely have seen Ewell's spitting on Atticus as more ominous, even if Scout did not. Miss Stephanie's closing observation on Atticus, "he could be right dry sometimes"— still indirect discourse, but her words, clearly—casts the incident in a droll and reassuring light. Lee, of course, chose the line for this reason.

Indirect discourse is your way of controlling the storyteller, and the story.

Indirect discourse is your way of controlling the storyteller, and the story. What light do you want to cast the story in? How quickly do you want to tell it? You can shorten it to a sentence or two, or let it run. You can throw in a little of the storyteller's idiom. You can add some dialogue. Think of it as a collaboration between you and the storyteller, but remember that you are the one in control.

7

DIALECT, ACCENTS, AND THE VERNACULAR

IMPARTING DIALECT

The opening of Faulkner's *Light in August*:

> Sitting beside the road, watching the wagon mount the hill toward her, Lena thinks, 'I have come from Alabama: a fur piece. All the way from Alabama a-walking. A fur piece.' Thinking although I have not been quite a month on the road I am already in Mississippi, further from home than I have ever been before. I am now further from Doane's Mill than I have been since I was twelve years old.

Lena Grove's journey is a search for the man whose child she's carrying. The kindly Armstids take her in for the night, and in the morning Mr. Armstid takes her in his wagon to Varner's Store:

> She rises and walking a little awkwardly, a little carefully, she traverses the ranked battery of maneyes and enters the store, the clerk following. 'I'm a-going to do it,' She thinks, even while ordering the cheese and crackers; 'I'm a-going to do it,' saying aloud: "And a box of sardines." She calls them sour-deens. "A nickel box."
> "We ain't got no nickel sardines," the clerk says. "Sardines is fifteen cents." He also calls them sour-deens.

A fur piece and *sour-deens* are all the help Faulkner gives us in hearing the honeyed drawl of the deep South in the voice of Lena Grove, and of other poor whites like the store clerk. It's enough. Lena buys the sardines and another good-hearted stranger gives her a ride into the town of Jefferson. She questions him:

> "I reckon you don't know anybody in Jefferson named Lucas Burch."
>
> "Burch?"
>
> "I'm looking to meet him there. He works at the planing mill."
>
> "No," the driver says, "I don't know that I know him. But likely there is a right smart of folks in Jefferson I don't know. Likely he is there."
>
> "I'll declare, I hope so. Travelling is getting right bothersome."

Hear the softness in Lena's voice, the elongations? Faulkner, with no more than *a fur piece* and *sour-deens*, has alerted us to the accent in Lena's speech. He doesn't reproduce her pronunciation again in the novel. He doesn't have to; he has set her dialogue to music.

• • •

Lena Grove is poor and uneducated. The clerk in Varner's is from the same hardscrabble milieu. Armstid, a dirt farmer, says "sho" for "sure," which marks his dialogue in the same way "a fur piece" marks Lena's.

Now listen to Jason Compson and his mother, in the third section of *The Sound and the Fury*, narrated by the odious Jason:

> "She didn't go to school today," she says. "I just know she didn't. She says she went for a car ride with one of the boys this afternoon and you followed her."
>
> "How could I?" I says. "When somebody had my car all afternoon? Whether or not she was in school today is already

past," I says. "If you've got to worry about it, worry about next Monday."

"I wanted you and she to get along with one another," she says. "But she has inherited all of the headstrong traits. Quentin's too. I thought at the time with the heritage she would already have, to give her that name, too. Sometimes I think she is the judgment of both of them upon me."

"Good Lord," I says. "You've got a fine mind. No wonder you keep yourself sick all the time."

The Compsons are gentry, though they've fallen on hard times, and Faulkner writes their dialogue in *The Sound and the Fury* and *Absalom, Absalom!* with no indication of an accent. In *Light in August* he does the same with the dialogue of Joe Christmas, the tormented protagonist. Christmas is an orphan, drifter, moonshiner, and finally a murderer, but there's a worldliness about him, he's been around, and his dialogue comes without the rural caress and backwoods melody of Lena's. The dialogue of the seminary-educated minister, Gail Hightower, is unaccented. All of these Mississippians, of course, are speaking with what any northerner would hear as a distinct southern accent.

Major de Spain and General Compson, in "The Bear," are Confederate veterans and country aristocrats, and their dialogue is almost formal, reflecting their standing as educated men and landowners. They're planning the day's pursuit—yet again—of the gigantic grizzly, Big Ben:

"We'll put General Compson on Katie this morning," Major de Spain said. "He drew blood last year; if he'd had a mule then would have stood, he would have—"

"No," General Compson said. "I'm too old to go helling through the woods on a mule or a horse or anything else anymore. Besides, I had my chance last year and missed it. I'm going on a stand this morning. I'm going to let that boy ride Katie."

There's a pattern here. Faulkner allocates an accent, or doesn't, according to social class. His black characters—servants or laborers a couple of generations removed from slavery, if that—speak a dialect of their own, with an accent written into every line of their dialogue. Dilsey and her son, Luster:

> "Whut you up to" she said.
> "Nothin," Luster said. "Mr. Jason say fer me to find out whar dat water leak in de cellar fum."
> "En when wus hit he say fer you do do dat?" Disley said. "Last New Year's day, wasn't hit?"
> "I thought I jes be lookin whiles dey sleep," Luster said.

Wash Jones, Thomas Sutpen's white retainer in the eponymous short story, which, retold, became a key event in *Absalom, Absalom!*, is so low-born and ignorant that even Sutpen's former slaves look down on him. Few of Faulkner's poor whites speak as colloquially as Wash:

> "I ain't afraid. Because you air brave. It ain't that you were
> a brave man at one minute or day in your life and got a paper to
> show hit from General Lee. But you air brave, the same as you air
> alive and breathing . . . And I know that whatever you handle or
> tech, whether hit's a regiment of men or a ignorant gal or just a
> hound dog, that you will make hit right."

Air for *are, tech* for *touch, hit's* for *it's*—nobody else in the story, *Wash,* or in *Absalom, Absalom!* speaks quite like Wash, who is one of Faulkner's more poignant characters. His dialogue is straitened, like his life, the diction cramped: the voice of the poor white South.

Like Faulkner, most southern writers give their dialogue an accent, or don't, depending on social class. In Pete Dexter's southern gothic novel, *Paris Trout,* the dialogue of Trout's educated wife, Hanna—and of the lawyer, Townes, and the county prosecutor, Seagraves—is uninflected, while Trout's diction is just imperfect enough to convey his country upbringing and the flavor of an accent. The accents in *Paris Trout* broaden farther down the social ladder. A white policeman brings the young black girl, Rosie Sayers, home, after she's been bitten by a fox:

> "Miz Sayers," the police was saying, "I am Officer Andrews, and I brung you something home."
> The girl's mother looked around the police until she saw her. "What's she did?"
> The police's head moved back until a roll of skin formed over his collar. "Nothin'," he said. "But a white lady fetched her to the clinic onaccount she said she been bit by something."

Something to notice: the southern accent in this colloquy is implicit. It resides not in phonetic spellings that alter pronunciation—except, perhaps for *Miz*—but in the syntax and grammatical irregularities. *Brung, What's she did?, onaccount:* they have a languid, country sound that we hear as southern. They *read* accented.

The southern characters in Lee Smith's *Family Linen* are solidly middle class, and their dialogue, too, is uninflected. But it's different among the folks of the Virginia hill country. *Oral History* spans three generations, going back to a time of extreme isolation and want in southern Appalachia, and the dialogue in the first half of the novel is the most colloquial and accented in Smith's fiction. Early in the novel, Granny Younger—midwife, herbalist, and clairvoyant—counsels Almarine Cantrell, who has come under the spell of the beautiful Red Emmy. Red Emmy, according to local lore, is a witch. Granny Younger is narrating:

> "They's something else," Almarine said.
> "They's always something else," I said.
> "She's gonner have a baby," Almarine says. He cries down into his hands.

> "Good God in heaven," I say. "It won't be no baby like none of us-uns ever seed, I'll tell you that. You get rid of her, Almarine," what I told him, "afore you get a passel of witch children up there."

Almarine and Granny Younger are speaking what amounts to an indigenous language—a dialect. *They's, gonner,* and *afore* aren't intrinsically southern pronunciations, but the exotic idiom and diction of this dialogue conjure a remote time and place, a bygone language, spoken in an accent more imagined than heard.

The members of Smith's musical family in *The Devil's Dream,* which also encompasses three generations, get around more and are less provincial than the hillbillies in *Oral History.* Even among the early generations, their idiom is less eccentric and more modern:

> "If you are going with me," Daddy said as we started off that evening, "I don't want to hear no whining, nor no muley-mouthing, nor nothing like it, from either one of you girls. I don't want to hear nobody say, 'Daddy, I'm so tired.' Nor do I want to hear nothing spoke about nobody taking a little sip."

There's backcountry in this speech, with its errant verb forms and double negatives. Notice, however, that the spelling is conventional; Smith relies on syntax to give her dialogue an accent, using words like musical notes and arranging them along the line to produce the melody of the region. Late in the same novel, Ralph Handy gives Katie Cocker a pep talk:

> "Well, now, I'm just a old country boy," Ralph Handy said—he always said this!—"but I ain't so sure about that. What it looks to me like, he owes you a lot. He's in your debt, and not the other way round, and don't you forget it, honey. It's your songs."

I'm just a old country boy sounds like a lyric at the Grand Ole Opry and probably was, more than once. Consider the difference between *What it looks like to me* and Ralph Handy's rendition, *What it looks to me like*. The transposition of that one word, *like*, changes the sound of the phrase. It gives it a lift at the end and keeps *like* on the tongue a fraction longer, opening the word out, giving it a twang. *It's your songs* is one of those lines of dialogue that looks easy to write and are not. Maybe Smith heard it somewhere, maybe she concocted it herself. Either way, it sounds just like that old country boy, Ralph Handy.

Ralph and the singer Blackjack Johnny Raines couldn't be more different, the one loving and wise, the other a liar and a hustler, but you wouldn't know it from the sweet sound of Johnny's voice. He's coming on to a floozy he picked up in a bar:

> "Honey, I've gotta come right out and say something to you. When I saw you sitting in that bar back there, I can't tell you what come over me, the way I felt, I mean. You look just like my sister, I swear you do. You look just like she would of looked if she'd ever of growed up, I mean."

We know what Johnny is up to, and the woman suspects it. She'll go with him, though. There's honey in the voice, something smooth and easygoing. The words fall in quaint patterns, like the lyrics of a country song. *I can't tell you what come over me, the way I felt, I mean.* Who doesn't love a southern accent?

• • •

Outside of the South, novelists generally ignore regional accents. In almost any fiction—take your pick—the dialogue of a character from Indiana, say, reads pretty much like that of a character from Pennsylvania. Didion's Californians pronounce their words, as far we can tell, the same way Anne Tyler's Baltimoreans pronounce theirs. John Cheever's New Yorkers sound just like his New Englanders.

A New England accent is distinctive, but most writers leave it alone in their dialogue. (Do *not* let your grizzled Cape Codder or Maine fisherman call a northeast storm a "nor'easter," which is an invention of television meteorologists. The old Yankees didn't pronounce their r's; "nawth-easter," they said.) The dialogue in *The Friends of Eddie Coyle* is packed with local references—the Bruins, Logan Airport, MCI Walpole—but Higgins leaves pronunciation to the reader and, references aside, these guys could be crooks and lawmen in Miami. The crime writer Dennis Lehane and the mystery writer Robert B. Parker set their fiction in and around Boston, and their dialogue is as uninflected as Hemingway's, and nearly as good.

John Sayles, curiously, gives his Bostonians a broad and explicit New England accent in *Union Dues*. The two protagonists, young Hobie McNatt and his father, Hunter, have traveled up separately from West Virginia, Hobie searching for his older brother, Hunter searching for Hobie. The McNatts live in the hills, coal country, but Sayles gives their dialogue no accent; the New England accents, maybe, are a testament to the foreignness of Boston to Hobie and Hunter.

Hobie has fetched up in a commune. One of the residents is a young ex-boxer named King:

"... I'm in the quatter finals. I'm gonna fight this kid, Pawto Rican kid from the South End, he's sposed to take the whole thing. I get by him, I'm golden, prawbly I can coast the rest of the way."

Hunter meets a divorcee named Helen, who admires him for leaving home, at his age, for an uncertain future. She couldn't do it, Helen says:

"I'm pretty tied down here. There's the girls, they got their friends and I wouldn't think of pulling them out of St. Brigid's.

It's so hod to find a decent school you stot moving around. Then there's this house, I got the mawgage to keep up with . . ."

I'm a lifelong New Englander, and it's true that a lot of us sound like King and Helen. But regional accents, which are common in everyday speech, almost universal, are disproportionate in their effect on dialogue in fiction. New Englanders like Helen may say *hod* for *hard*, *stot* for *start*, and *mawgage* for *mortgage*, but the written words are intrusive. (*Mawgage* sounds like a squawk.) They call attention to themselves at the expense of the rest of the line. They distract the reader.

Sayles's short story, *Hoop*, written earlier, is also set in Boston, but the dialogue is undoctored. The story is about a high school basketball player who receives counsel in the ways of the world from his father and other loiterers in a South Boston bar and pool room:

> "You keep your eyes open, boy, opportunity is everywhere." The old man never turned, but talked to Brian by way of the mirror over the bar. "Twenty years on the railroad and never once did I ask myself where those loads, those trains, were heading. That's where it was, and I never went after it. Right under my nose and there I was, too blind to smell it."
>
> "What your father means, Sport, is you go where the action is. You settle for what you got and life passes you by."
>
> "Wasted my youth on a dead-end job. And youth, youth you never get back."

The clean dialogue in *Hoop* gets the undistracted reading it deserves. *The Sound and the Fury* and *Absalom, Absalom!* will soon be a hundred years old; their dialects, surely accurate, would seem overdone today. Be wary of improvised spellings as a way of giving dialogue an accent; they can be distracting. An evocative and timely colloquialism, woven into an imaginative syntax, work just as well, or better.

INDICATING FOREIGN ACCENTS

Hunter McNatt has found a factory job, and his Italian co-workers are discussing current events during a lunch break in *Union Dues*:

> "You see what a Presiden say?"
>
> "I don' rememb."
>
> "Presiden Neex, ee say soon no mo gasoline. No mo automobile. Evvabody buy sick."
>
> "Che?"
>
> "Buy sick. Bicicletta."
>
> "That so?"
>
> "Ee said eemself. Alla price go up. Evvating coast too much. Groun beef, dolar a poun. Forget it."
>
> "Where you go buy?"
>
> Stope anna Shope"
>
> "You go to Gran Yoon, is jus as good."
>
> "Not what they say onna TV."
>
> "You gonna bleeve evvating they say? Listen a me, I'm go to Gran Yoon five, seex year now. Jus as good."

This phonetic tour de force by John Sayles is one approach to foreign accents. This time Sayles hits the jackpot; it's wonderful dialogue—antic and unpredictable. Sayles writes it to make us smile, even when the tyrannical foreman, Puglisi, is talking:

> "What you do?"
>
> "Huh?"
>
> "You hens! Get em outa you pocket. I don't care what you do with, jus you nev' let me catch you with hens in you pocket."

I think Sayles's ear is dead-on here, but the authenticity of the dialogue is beside the point. It *sounds* authentic; if it didn't, it would fall embarrassingly flat, like an unfunny standup comedian. Sayles takes a gamble here—he was twenty-seven when he wrote *Union Dues*—and gets away with it.

Be careful.

The dialogue of Sayles's Italians—even Puglisi's bullying—works as comic relief. The Italians appear only briefly in the novel; Sayles knows better than to fill a book with dialogue as jerrybuilt and syntactically unruly as this. It can be funny for only so long.

I had a French uncle who spoke fluent English, and as a child I loved listening to him speak. I loved his softened consonants, his mellifluous vowels. My aunt's name was Julia: *Zhulia*, he called her. Boston was *Boh-stun*, Hemingway, whom he read in English, was *Heh-meeng-way.*

If there's a foreigner in your novel, think hard about his or her dialogue. To write the actual sound of my uncle's Frenchified speech you would have to alter the English spelling of nearly every word, as Sayles does with the dialogue of his Italians. Over the long haul, and even the short one, this has a disruptive effect: it requires some getting used to, every time, and it gives the lines a gloss that can hog the reader's attention. Sayles's Italianated words and phrases are such a delightful corruption of English that we don't pay much attention to what the others in the room are saying. That's okay—for a while.

There's a much less intrusive alternative to the heavy hand Sayles lays on the dialogue of his Italians. Just as you can evoke a southern accent by manipulating syntax and using the occasional colloquial word or expression, you can make a character from, say, France sound exotic and foreign. Dickens often overdoes accents, both regional and foreign, but he found just the right note in *Bleak House*, with the dialogue of the passionate and volatile Mademoiselle Hortense. Mademoiselle is an attractive woman with rage in her heart, and she is on a mission. She has come to the home of the lawyer Tulkinghorn, who has been employing her in a dark scheme of his own:

"I have had great deal of trouble to find you, sir."

"Have you!"

"I have been here very often, sir. It has always been said to me, he is not at home, he is engage, he is not for you."

"Quite right, and quite true."

"Not true. Lies!"

"Now, mistress," says the lawyer, tapping the key hastily on the chimney-piece. "If you have anything to say, say it, say it."

"Sir, you have not use me well. You have been mean and shabby."

"Mean and shabby, eh?" returns the lawyer.

"Yes. What is it that I tell you? You know you have. You have attrapped me—catched me—to give you information . . ."

Spell Check nails only two words here, *attrapped* and *catched,* and neither is a phonetic rendering (Hortense probably says *cotched*). Dickens spoke French and knew how certain literal translations would come out in English: *he is not for you, What is it that I tell you?* There are other, slighter syntactical oddities: *It has always been said to me.* Dickens drops the "d" from Hortense's past participles. My Swiss uncle didn't use contractions—"I have not the time," he said—and Mademoiselle doesn't, either. She says Tulkinghorn has been "mean" and "shabby," expressive words which don't quite fit the case.

Dickens, then, gives Hortense a French accent by implication. He spells conventionally, but plays with her grammar and syntax. Reading her dialogue, you can't help sounding French, just as you can't help sounding southern when you read Ralph Handy's.

Irwin Shaw didn't speak German when he wrote his famous short story, *Sailor off the Bremen,* in 1939, but there's a crispness, an economy and feel of rigidity, in the dialogue of the Nazi Lueger, the steward who has been lured ashore by a woman in New York:

"That was a very fine film tonight," Lueger was saying. "I enjoy Deanna Durbin. Very young, fresh sweet. Like you."

It helps to know the language of your foreigner. There's a diverse cast of Mexicans in McCarthy's Border Trilogy, with a varying command of English. In *All the Pretty Horses* John Grady Cole is being questioned by the captain after his and Rawlins' arrest:

The peoples in this town are quiet peoples. Everybody here is quiet all the time.

He leaned forward and stubbed out the cigarette in the ashtray.

Then comes the assassin Blevins to steal horses and kill everybody. Why is this? He was a quiet boy and never do no harm and then he come here and do these things something like that?

He leaned back and shook his head in that same sad way.

No, he said. He wagged one finger. No.

He watched John Grady.

What is the truth is this: He was no quiet boy. He was this other kind of boy all the time. All the time.

The captain muddles his verb tenses and subject-verb agreement. He uses double negatives. But amid all this grammatical chaos, everything is spelled correctly, as if it were a point of honor with McCarthy to keep every word intact. Notice, too, that the Captain doesn't use contractions. Foreigners speaking English tend not to, and it's an easy way to enhance the unnatural melody and cadence of their dialogue.

The captain's Spanish accent seems embedded in his flawed English: the flaws sound like errant translations, and in them we hear, or imagine we do, a skewed pronunciation. But the vicious pimp, Eduardo, in *Cities of the Plain*, speaks perfect, even elegant, English, and it is McCarthy's disposition of his words that gives his dialogue an accent, both Spanish and oily. Billy Parham has come to the brothel bringing John Grady's offer to buy the prostitute, Magdalena:

> Your friend is in the grip of an irrational passion, Eduardo said. Nothing you say to him will matter. He has in his head a certain story. Of how things will be. In this story he will be happy. What is wrong with this story?
>
> You tell me.
>
> What is wrong with this story is that it is not a true story. Men have in their minds a picture of how he world will be. How they will be in that world. The world may be many different ways for them but there is one world that will never be and that is the world they dream of.

I've said that dialogue must be unpredictable—that every speech should, if only in a mild way, surprise us. Eduardo's syntax and diction can't be faulted at any point, and yet nearly every line contains some peculiarity in its construction. Direct objects don't immediately follow transitive verbs. Words are repeated when their antecedent is clear—*story, dream*—as if Eduardo enjoys their sound. It isn't just Eduardo's speeches that are unpredictable; it is his sentence structure. His diction is unusual—elaborate, inventive, polished. It is unmistakably foreign.

USING THE VERNACULAR

Consider the sentence, "I'm going to fool him." What does it sound like when you read it to yourself? When you read it aloud? What would it sound like if you spoke it to a friend, in an unheated or casual conversation? I'm an educated man with a high regard for linguistic propriety, and I would say, conversationally, "I'm gonna fool him." I would not pronounce the *g*, and *to* would be mashed down to a vague *a* or *uh*.

I bet you would do the same. Who doesn't? College professors, ballplayers, construction workers, writers: do any of us pronounce "going to" as it's written, say, in "I'm going to fool him," or "She's going to be sorry," or "You're going to wish you'd listened to me"?

We don't. Not usually. So should we write dialogue this way? Never? Sometimes? If so, when?

Here's the opening of Hemingway's short story *Fifty Grand*, about the aging prizefighter, Jack Brennan:

> "How are you going yourself, Jack?" I asked him.
>
> "You seen this Walcott?" he says.
>
> "Just in the gym."
>
> "Well," says Jack, "I'm going to need a lot of luck with that boy."
>
> "He can't hit you, Jack," Soldier said.
>
> "I wish to hell he couldn't."
>
> "He couldn't hit you with a handful of bird-shot."
>
> "Bird-shot'd be all right," Jack says. "I wouldn't mind bird-shot any."
>
> "He looks easy to hit," I said.
>
> "Sure," Jack says, "he ain't going to last long. He ain't going to last like you and me, Jerry. But right now he's got everything."

Three times Jack Brennan says "going to," not "gonna," and even so, Jack's dialogue sounds as real and raw as any you'll read. Hemingway is the inventor of modern dialogue, and it was his genius that enabled him to write hard-edged, colloquial-sounding dialogue without resorting to altered spellings like "gonna." All of the dialogue in *Fifty Grand* is worth reading: the brief speeches, the one-syllable words, the quick, erratic rhythms. There's tension and a sour dissonance pervading every speech. Jack Brennan is entering the ring at Madison Square Garden for the fight that is the story's climax:

> Jack climbed up and bent down to go through the ropes and Walcott came over and pushed the rope down for Jack to go through.

The crowd thought that was wonderful. Walcott put his hand on Jack's shoulder and they stood there just for a second.

"So you're going to be one of those popular champions," Jack says to him. "Take your goddamn hand off my shoulder."

The "So" at the front of the first line, rather than softening it—there's no comma after it; a comma would give the line a hesitancy, turn it cautious—floods it with disdain. *I see you're going to be one of those . . .* it says. You can see Jack's lip curl. The following line is abrupt, overtly hostile. The expletive gives it the force of a blow. The speech *sounds* tough; who notices "going to?"

I have a theory about Hemingway: he was so devoted to language, so averse to corrupting it in any way, that he set himself the task of achieving the effect of "gonna" without writing it. Consider this the ideal, meet it when you can, and use "gonna," or some equivalent, only when it seems necessary.

• • •

The idlers in the "one-horse" Arkansas town in *Huckleberry Finn* speak one of the several dialects, probably "Pike County," described by Twain in his "Explanation" at the front of the book. They're sitting under awnings, whittling, chewing tobacco, when the drunken buffoon, Boggs, comes galloping into town:

All the loafers looked glad; I reckoned they was used to having fun out of Boggs. One of them says:

"Wonder who he's a-gwyne to chaw up this time. If he'd a-chawed up all the men he's ben a-gwyne to chaw up in the last twenty year he'd have considerable ruputation now."

Another one says, "I wisht old Boggs'd threaten me, 'cuz then I'd know I warn't gwyne to die for a thousan' year."

Boggs comes a-tearing along on his horse, whooping and yelling like an Injun, and singing out:

"Clear the track, thar. I'm on the waw-path, and the price uv coffins is a-gwyne to raise."

Hemingway called *Huckleberry Finn* America's "best book," so he presumably had no objection to the flamboyant inventiveness of its dialogue, which is so unlike the surgical precision of his own. "Going to," in the Arkansas loafers' parlance, becomes "a-gwyne to." Twain paints these men as degenerates—"an ornery lot"—and loads their dialogue with mispronunciations and grammatical eccentricities, giving it a reek of ignorance and idle malice. (They sic dogs on pigs, and light dogs on fire with turpentine for their amusement.) Boggs is as ignorant, if not as mean, as they, and speaks the same language.

Boggs hollers threats at store owner, Colonel Sherburn, who comes out and gives him an ultimatum, effective in fifteen minutes. Boggs continues his drunken rant. Sherburn returns, shoots him dead, and goes back inside. The loafers talk themselves into forming a lynch mob, and in one of the novel's great scenes, Sherburn, cool and contemptuous, confronts them with a shotgun from the gallery roof of his store. Twain uses "going to" in Sherburn's withering disquisition to the crowd, which goes, in part:

"You don't like trouble and danger. But if only half a man—like Buck Harkness, there—shouts 'Lynch him! lynch him!' you're afraid to back down—afraid you'll be found out to be what you are—cowards—and so you raise a yell, and hang yourselves onto that half-a-man's coat-tail, and come raging up here, swearing what big things you're going to do. The pitifulest thing out is a mob; that's what an army is—a mob; they don't fight with courage that's born in them, but with courage that's borrowed from their mass, and from their officers. But a mob without any man at the head of it is beneath pitifulness. Now the thing for you to do is to droop your tails and go home and crawl in a hole. If any real lynching's going to be done it will be done in the dark, Southern fashion; and when they come they'll bring their masks, and fetch a man along . . ."

The speech is a page and a half long, and its diction establishes Sherburn as educated and, in a cold-blooded way, genteel. Twain was as aware as you and I that even people as refined as Colonel Sherburn say "gonna," but he was making a distinction here between Sherburn and the bumpkin mob. The choice, "going to" or "gonna," matters.

William Kennedy's *Ironweed* protagonist, Francis Phelan, says "gonna," his voice and diction roughened by age and hard knocks, as well as a meager education. So do his pals and fellow bums. But Francis's off-and-on-again girlfriend, Helen Archer, who has descended to dereliction and homelessness from the upper middle class and Smith College, says "going to." The cultivated and beautiful—and finally mad—Katrina Daugherty, who appears briefly but significantly in *Ironweed* and is the female protagonist of *The Flaming Corsage*, says "going to."

Scout Finch, getting taunted in the schoolyard, says, "You gonna take that back, boy?" And when a man grabs her brother roughly by the collar: "Ain't nobody gonna do Jem that way." But Scout speaks more articulately when she gets on Atticus's lap after he has taken on the case of Tom Robinson. Atticus advises her:

> "You might hear some ugly talk about it at school, but do one thing for me if you will: you just hold your head high and keep those fists down. No matter what anybody says to you, don't let 'em get your goat. Try fighting with your head for a change . . . it's a good one, even if it does resist learning."
>
> "Atticus, are we going to win?"
>
> "No, honey."

The question and its answer comprise one of the novel's many poignant moments, and "gonna" would weaken it. Scout is working out a profound moral perplexity, and she's speaking thoughtfully, slowly. "Going to" is commensurate with the moment.

• • •

To read Cormac McCarthy's dialogue is to understand that syntactical touchups like *gonna* for *going to* are as much about the visual—the appearance of the printed words—as about the sound. The absence in McCarthy's novels of quotation marks, commas, and apostrophes— *dont* for *don't*, *cant* for *can't*—makes no difference if you hear them read aloud; McCarthy writes for the eye as well as the ear.

John Grady Cole is talking to his boss, Mac McGovern, in *Cities of the Plain*:

> What were you goin to say?
> That's all right.
> You can say it. Go ahead.
> Well, I guess I was goin to say that I didnt think I could keep him out of trouble on no part time basis.

Read this aloud. Your tongue barely clicks on the *t* in *goin to*, if it clicks at all. But the *to* is conspicuous to the eye. *Goin to*: it's McCarthy's *gonna*, with a visual difference. It's precise. It's tidy.

Here's another exchange between John Grady Cole and Mac McGovern in *Cities*:

> You dont know or you aint sayin?
> I dont know. If I wasn't sayin I'd of said so.
> I know you would.
> Sir.
> Yes.
> I feel kind of bad about Delbert.
> What do you feel bad about?
> I guess I feel like I took his job.
> Well you didnt. He'd of been gone anyways.

I'd of said so and I'd have said so sound the same, but they don't read the same.

I'd of said so, I'd have said so. He'd of been gone, he'd have been gone. Read them aloud: there's no difference. You can't broaden the *o* in *of* without warping the sentence. *I'd of said so* and *I'd have said so* sound the same, but they don't *read* the same. *Of* for *have* in the conditional tense is a purely visual device that conveys, or represents, a plainness or lack of sophistication in the diction of the speaker. It's a signal.

In *Seen the Glory*, Elisha Smith, a semi-educated Martha's Vineyard farm boy, says *would of.* So do the hayseed Virginia twins, Lilac and Iris, who may not be literate. My thought, writing their dialogue, was that the characters themselves aren't aware of a distinction between *would of* and *would have.* Maybe they *mean* to say *would of.* Maybe they mean to say *would have.* Maybe they don't know the difference. Whichever, their grammar is rudimentary, and *would of* says so, in writing.

• • •

Dave Foley, the federal agent in *The Friends of Eddie Coyle*, is conversing with a colleague:

> "That's what made me wonder," Dave said. "I dunno whether Eddie Fingers is telling me all he knows about the militants or not."

Foley is talking to Eddie:

> "I'll be right here."
> "No," Coyle said. "I wanta see you, make sure I know everything that's going on."

Eddie again:

> "You said you hadda have a reason. So I give you a reason."

As with "would of," the effect of these contractions and compressions of two words into one is visual. Say "I don't know" or "I want to see you" as if you were speaking to your spouse, your kid, a colleague at work—say them right now, out loud, conversationally—and you hear yourself say *dunno* and *wanta. Hadda* is more robust and distinctive; most of us don't coarsen *had to* to *hadda,* but how distinctly do we usually pronounce the *o* in *had to?*

The characters in *Eddie Coyle* are without affectation, to say the least, and *dunno, wanta, hadda,* and so on give their dialogue a careless aspect. They tell us that these guys are indifferent to how they sound. *I wanta go:* we say it all the time, but to read it is to hear that indifference in the voices—an indifference to etiquette, social norms, the ethics most people live by. Their dialogue is hard-edged. They have an urban toughness, a grit; these aren't country boys, by a long shot.

Hemingway won't misspell "going to," but his prizefighters, gangsters, and others on the outer edge of society say "ain't" and "don't" instead of "doesn't," and these common solecisms resonate through all of their dialogue. They go a long way, in other words. Begin with them when your character is semi-educated or otherwise rough around the edges, and from there decide how much tinkering you want to do with his or her grammar and pronunciation—if any.

• • •

The tricks vary from author to author. Jaxon Dunmire, the cowboy turned windmill salesman, is soliciting a distant neighbor in Annie Proulx's short story, *People In Hell Just Want A Drink of Water.*

"Mr. Tinsley? Howdy. Jax Dunmire. Meaning a come out here for two years and persuade you about the Mornin Glory windmill. Probably the best equipment on the market and the mill that's saving the rancher's bacon these damn dustbowl days. Yeah, I been meanin a get out here, but I been so damn busy at the ranch and

then runnin up and down the state summers sellin these good mills
I don't get around the home territory much." The smile lay over his
face as if it had been screwed on. "My dad and my brothers and
me, we got five a these Mornin Glories on the Rockin Box."

Meaning to get out here becomes *meanin a get out here,* which is
conspicuous on the page but not so very far from the way most of us
would say it, speaking normally. It looks colloquial, is the point. Say *Five of
these,* casually, and it sounds a lot like *five a these.* It might sound just like it.

"I find out this fella runs a sports book, loves the game of baseball
and has a head fulla stats," says Chickasaw Charlie Hoke in Leonard's
eponymous short story.

"It hurt a lotta bums," says Francis Phelan's pal, Rudy. "Ain't many
of the old ones left."

"I still say he shoulda kept his mouth shut," says the barbershop
loafer, Freddie, in Song of Solomon.

Head fulla stats. Lotta bums. Shoulda kept his mouth shut. We all say
these things in real life, but when you write them they characterize
your dialogue in a very specific way. They become vernacular.

• • •

The dialogue in *The Friends of Eddie Coyle* was, at the time,
revolutionary. No one had read anything like it—Higgins had a
new agent; his previous agent had said he wouldn't be able to sell
the novel, and dropped him—and no one has quite duplicated
it. I wouldn't try to copy George V. Higgins; constant syntactical
touchups like *dunno* and *wanta* can become overly conspicuous to
the reader, if not plain annoying. Higgins incorporated them into
his dialogue so skillfully and thoroughly—he makes *words* out of
them—that they quickly become natural to his characters. We can't
imagine them talking any other way. Higgins turned *wanta* and
dunno into gold and gave the vernacular of the underworld literary
respectability; Elmore Leonard acknowledged a debt to him. It's

hard to imagine Proulx's odd but convincing colloquialisms before Higgins broke the ground he did.

Emulate these masters, borrow from them, steal—it is what writers do—but with caution. Remember how distinctive, in a line of dialogue, these phonetic contrivances are, and save them for the cowboys and their wives, the crooks, the molls, the hard-bitten cops, the hicks, the waitresses in hash houses, the prostitutes and strippers. Do *not* have your Wellesley College English major say "gonna" because kids talk that way, or because she's excited, or in an effusive mood. It's the wrong message to the reader—a visual message. And remember that one *hadda,* or *wanta,* or *shoulda* too many can be ruinous, for the very reason you use them: the reader notices.

• • •

And then there is language that does change the sound, as well as the look, of a line.

A for *an* suggests an imperfect education. "Don't be a ass," Rawlins says in *All the Pretty Horses.* "They are callin our place a entertainment ranch," says Cody Joe Bibby in Proulx's story, *Pair A Spurs.* I used it in *Seen the Glory* as standard speech for characters from the backcountry and small, poor towns. "You don't want a Enfield rifle," Elisha Smith says. Lilac Purdy, the country prostitute, asks Thomas Chandler, "Are you a abolitionist?"

It sounds more common than it probably is in real life. I don't recall ever hearing it, but so what? It sounds real—rustic and ignorant but not necessarily unintelligent.

Some years ago I came across a short story by Bo Ball entitled "It's Just One Elvis." The sentence struck me as both odd and interesting; in a moment I understood it was a colloquial rendering of "There's just one Elvis." The story is about a family pilgrimage to Graceland. It's comic and finally poignant, and the title introduces the protagonist, Galene, whose line of dialogue it is. Galene is a sexy young Tennessean, a wife and the mother of an adolescent boy named Son. She's an Elvis lover and the catalyst of this tragicomic odyssey:

> Galene teeth-hummed "Long Black Limousine." She twirled the radio dial onto a station that sounded a little country, a little rock. "It's just one Elvis," she said and shook her head at a grief now six years old.

It's Just One Elvis, the story and the line, stayed with me, and when the time came, there it was—made to order for Lilac and Iris Purdy, southern country girls, unlettered but shrewd, like Galene:

> ". . . with Pa gone it wasn't nobody to run the slaves and then some partisans come through and something happened, some argument, I guess, and next thing happened they hung one of em and took the other two off with em. They'd got right troublesome with no one to run em but what happened was pitiful, and we warn't no party to it. They hung the one and left him, and Iris and me helped his woman get him down and bury him. It wasn't no call to hang him."

This trick isn't for everyone. Lee Smith is generally averse to altered spellings and syntactical oddities and finds other ways, as we've seen, to evoke the backcountry speech of her mountain people, Proulx's rodeo riders and hard-luck ranchers don't say "would of," but McCarthy's young cowboys do.

• • •

It comes down to intuition. *It's just one Elvis:* look at it, listen to it—does it sound like your character? Does it give his or her dialogue the tone, the flavor, you're looking for? Does it hit a right note, or an off one? *It's just one Elvis.* Put it away and don't lose it. You never know.

• • •

**Improvise your
own vernacular.**

Improvise your own vernacular. I didn't invent
Elisha Smith; he did grow up on a farm on
Martha's Vineyard, and did enlist in the Union Army in 1861 at the age
of sixteen, as happens in my novel. Little is known of him—there are
no photographs—and I imagined the character with the help of several
letters he wrote in the weeks before Gettysburg. The letters reveal him
as earnest, sweet natured, and scantily educated. His mother had sent
him a cake, which he'd shared with his comrades, and he thanked her
for it and reported that they'd all enjoyed it: "The boys praised it up
very high."

I never found an occasion to use the line, but it was a gold mine
nevertheless. *Praised it up very high*: the adverbs are unorthodox as well as
redundant, and there's something quaint and homespun in their applica-
tion here that seemed to me to be the key to Elisha's dialogue. He isn't
good with words, but he isn't at a loss for them. The language in his
letters seemed improvised, slapped together, but expressive nevertheless.
In the novel the others are asleep, and Elisha and Thomas Chandler are
talking quietly the night before the regiment arrives in Gettysburg:

> "Got them scopes long as their gun barrels," Elisha said.
> "Infernal things. Put a ball between your eyes at half a mile." He
> unbuttoned his haversack. "Look what I got, Tommy. Been savin
> it." He lifted out a thick soft slab of something wrapped in news-
> paper. "It's cherry cake," he said. "Lady give it to me in Taneytown.
> We'll go halfs on it."
>
> "I ain't hungry," Thomas said.
>
> "You ain't hungry for cherry cake? Here." And he tore the limp
> wedge in two very gently and lifted a piece into Thomas's cupped
> hands.
>
> "She was a pretty lady give me this. Wore her hair down long.
> You didn't see her?"

"I might have."

Elisha brought his cake up with both hands and took a large bite. "Damn that's good," he said, with his mouth full. "Go on have you some, Tommy."

Thomas nodded. He took a bite of cake.

"Lady told me what it was," Elisha said, "or I wouldn't of known. Cherry cake. I never heard of such."

This last sentence was stolen from the great John Ford western, *The Searchers,* which I've seen more times than I like to admit. The circumstances are unimportant; the line, by a Texas rancher, is a vehement denial: "I never said that! I never said such!"

I was ten the first time I saw *The Searchers.* Not then, but somewhere over the years of repeated viewings, the line stayed with me. *Praised it up very high. Never said such.* Keep listening.

CONVEYING REGIONAL PATOIS

Huckleberry Finn has been attacked for its portrayal of Huck's companion Jim, the runaway slave. Jim's credulousness and super-stition, captured entirely in his dialogue (he never does a stupid or senseless thing) have been cited as racial stereotyping, a demeaning of African Americans.

These critics somehow miss one of the glaring truths of the novel. Huck's father is a drunken tramp and a bully. Miss Watson and the Widow Douglas are pious nitwits. The high-toned Shepherdsons and Grangerfords are waging a mindless blood feud. Colonel Sherburn is a cold-blooded killer. The Arkansas townsfolk are ignorant, idle, mean, and cowardly. The King and Duke are seedy swindlers and treacherous, to boot. If *Huckleberry Finn* demeans any race, it is the white one.

Jim occupies moral ground well above this rogues' gallery. Near the end of the novel he comes out of hiding to help the doctor remove the bullet from Tom Sawyer's leg, knowing he'll be recaptured.

Huck's belief in Jim is vindicated: "I was glad it was according to my judgment of him, too; because I thought he had a good heart in him and was a good man, the first time I seen him." No one else in the novel except, perhaps, the doughty Mary Jane Wilks, rates such deep respect from Huck, or Mark Twain, and we can dismiss the idea of Jim's speech as caricature.

Higgins's maxim that dialogue is character is every bit as true in *Huck Finn* as in *The Friends of Eddie Coyle*, and it is the content of Jim's dialogue, not its idiom, that defines him. He thinks of home and tells Huck about the time his four-year-old daughter, who had just recovered from scarlet fever, stood smiling at him when he asked her to close the door. He asked her again, and still she stood there, smiling:

> "En wid dat I fetch' her a slap side de head dat sont her a-sprawlin'. Den I went into de yuther room, en 'uz gone 'bout ten minutes; en when I come back day was dat do' a-stannin' open yit, en dat chile stannin' mos' right in it, a-lookin' down and mournin' en de tears runniun' down. My, but I wuz mad. I was a-gwyne for de chile, but jis' den— it was a do' dat open innerds—jis' den, 'long come de wind en slam it to, behine de chile, ker-blam!—en my lan', de child never move'! . . . Oh, Huck, I bust out a-cryin' en grab her up in my arms, en say, 'Oh, de po' little thing! De Lord God Almighty forgive po' ole Jim, kaze he never gwyne to fogive hisself as long's he live! Oh, she was plumb deef and dumb, Huck, plumb deef and dumb—en I'd ben a-treat'n her so!" . . .

Eighty years later came Styron's *Confessions of Nat Turner*. Nat is a preacher, steeped in the Bible and highly literate, and he speaks flawless English when he wants to. His fellow-slaves, condemned to illiteracy by law and convention, sound very much like Twain's Jim:

> "'Tain't nothing, Nat," he said weakly. "Hit jes' de misery I gits ev'y springtime. I gwine be awright come next week." After a pause he went on: "But nem'mine dat. Marse Samuel done told

me I gots to take dem four boys up to whar de trace begins at two
in de mawnin', What time hit now?"

Times change. Sensibilities change. However authentic Twain's and
Styron's slave dialects may be, they come across today as unnecessarily
inflected and ungrammatical. The escaped slaves living in Cincinnati
in Morrison's harrowing ghost story of a novel, *Beloved*, sound literate
by comparison. Here, Stamp Paid is trying to dissuade Baby Suggs,
worn out and grieving, from quitting preaching:

"You got to do it," he said. "You got to. Can't nobody call like you."
"What I have to do is get in my bed and lay down. I want to fix
on something harmless in this world."
"What world you talking about? Ain't nothing harmless down here."
"Yes it is. Blue. That don't hurt nobody. Yellow neither."
"You getting in the bed to think about yellow?"
"I likes yellow."
"Then what? When you get through with blue and yellow,
then what?"
"Can't say. It's something can't be planned."
"You blaming God," he said. "That's what you doing."
"No, Stamp. I ain't."

All of the major characters in *Beloved* are former slaves or their
children, and Morrison gives their dialogue a colloquial flavor without
Twain's and Styron's extreme idiom and manipulations of pronunciation. Morrison's characters—all reared in slavery, all in some way
damaged by it—speak a shared language. They don't sound colloquial
to each other, and Morrison wants the reader to hear them in the
same natural, grammatical-seeming way they hear each other.

You have a world of leeway, but never make the mistake of
equating dialect or vernacular with unintelligence. Jim isn't stupid,
and neither is Galene, in *It's Just One Elvis*. Eddie Coyle is as shrewd
as any professor across the river at Harvard. Colloquial speech, or

vernacular, is about time, place, and learning. It is the sound of where your characters come from.

TO CURSE OR NOT TO CURSE

There are no restrictions on profanity in fiction these days, as you surely know. The sky's the limit, but be judicious. Just because you *can* use an expletive doesn't mean you *should*. Profanities can work against, as well as for you.

The modern teenager and college student—even with the most genteel upbringing—typically garnishes his or her speech with expletives. Kids swear, and everybody knows it. So what about the kids in our novels?

A student of mine, the father of teenagers, was writing a novel— it was a good one—in which the male and female protagonists were fifteen. The girl had led a protected upper-middle class life. She went to a good school. Her father was a successful businessman. The boy's family was odd and dysfunctional but erudite; the boy, who was brought up on the water, could quote Melville and Joseph Conrad.

The dialogue was generally excellent, but after a while something began bothering me. It was the profanity: it felt randomly placed, gratuitous. It didn't sound like Travis and Christina. Their frequent expletives, sometimes angry, sometimes not, were projecting character that wasn't theirs. The words were giving out the wrong message.

Consider the implications of the words your characters use. The dialogue in *The Friends of Eddie Coyle* is laced with expletives. Crooks and lawmen alike use the "f" word constantly, usually in its adjectival form—their way of underlining a word. We understand that for them it is *de rigueur*—a password in the pragmatic and unforgiving world they inhabit. It's the only world they know, and the word comes naturally to them.

Where is your novel set? What circles do your characters move in? The profanity of the movie people in Didion's *Play It As It Lays* projects their life style; they live intemperately, they speak intemperately. They're flashy; profanity is flashy, it's hip. Didion's Hollywood is as predatory in its way as Eddie Coyle's Boston, and her characters speak an aggressive, abrasive language. McCarthy's cowboys swear, of course, but his women, who have an old-fashioned propriety, a dignity that brings out good manners in the men, don't. Proulx's women, on the other hand—ranch wives, female ropers, and honky-tonk prowlers—salt their speech with expletives.

Does Annabel, the Wellesley College junior in your novel, swear a blue streak when she finds out she failed chemistry? Okay, but if she does, it isn't because she's a college kid and all college kids swear; it's because she's Annabel, and Annabel has a notably foul mouth. Maybe obscenities for Annabel are a fashion statement, like loud lipstick or skirts halfway up her thigh. Maybe it's a feminist thing, a defiance of old boundaries. Maybe it's sheer mischief, Annabel's way of getting a rise out of people. Maybe there's anger, aggression in her cussing. Whatever the reason, her language can't be gratuitous. Dialogue, remember, reveals character.

Enjoy the freedom but use profanity artfully. An expletive can give a line of dialogue just the right touch of grit or earthy panache. It can give it a sawtooth edge. It can make it vehement, angry. It can even bring a smile. From *Eddie Coyle*:

> "You do not have to answer any questions," Moran said. "You have a right to remain silent. If you answer any questions, your answers may be used in evidence against you in a trial in a court of law. Do you understand what I have read to you?"
>
> "Of course I understand," Jackie Brown said. "You think I'm a fucking idiot?"

Allow your characters to swear, but don't force them to.

Allow your characters to swear, but don't force them to.

All dialogue is an invented language, and colloquial speech, vernacular, is your license to turn your imagination loose. Look for words in odd conjunction as you write. Invent your own grammatical oddities and solecisms. Some extravagance is okay.

Keep your sense of humor. The proprietor of Slick's Bar and Grill on the south side of Chicago, Alphaeus Jones, produces a shotgun from under the counter when two racketeers posing as community organizers come in to shake him down in James Alan McPherson's short story, *The Silver Bullet:*

> Now R.V.'s lips curled into a confident grin. He shook his head several times. "Let me run something down for you, brother," he said. "First of all, we're a nonprofit community-based grass-roots organization, totally responsive to the needs of the community. Second"—and here he again brought his fingers into play—"we think the community would be very interested in the articulation of the total proceeds of this joint vis-à-vis the average income level for this area. Third, you don't want to mess with us. We got the support of college students."
>
> "Do tell," Jones said. "Well, I ain't never been to college myself, but I can count to ten. And if you punks ain't down the block when I finish, that street out there is gonna be full of hamburger meat."

Venacular can't sparkle in every line, but often it will. Don't pass up the chance.

8

GREAT LINES: WHY I LOVE TO WRITE DIALOGUE

Dialogue is an art form, and it surprises me that so many writers, even successful ones, don't rely on it more than they do. This is personal: I'll grant that fiction can be good without a lot of dialogue, but the choice not to write dialogue seems inscrutable to me. Dialogue is as useful as you want it to be; get along without it if you can, but why would you want to? It's so much fun to write!

"It is always the person not in the predicament who knows what ought to have been done in it," Dickens observes in an aside in *A Christmas Carol,* "and would unquestionably have done it too."

Dickens could have been describing the pleasure of writing dialogue. How many times have you wished you, or someone with you, had spoken up? Afterward, you hit on the astute remark, the apt wisecrack, the withering rejoinder, which would have turned a dull or one-sided exchange into something worth telling. *I should have said . . . I wish he'd told that nosy cop to . . . If only she'd stood up and . . .* Your story or novel is your chance. Our characters, depending on who they are, don't always say the smart thing, the brave thing, the witty thing, the poignant thing, but whatever they say is what they *ought* to have said, to paraphrase Dickens. And when they do make the apt wisecrack or that withering rejoinder, the satisfaction is as real as if you'd said it yourself.

Your characters have to respond immediately, but you have all the time you need to craft that response.

Whatever our characters say, we write their dialogue with a freedom amounting to the hindsight Dickens is talking about. The freedom is time to think about what your character is going to say. "Proceed slowly, and take care," advises Annie Proulx. A good line of dialogue might take twenty minutes to sketch out, shape, and fine tune. Your characters have to respond immediately, but you have all the time you need to craft that response. Take the time. Don't be in a hurry.

My wife, who is a reader, says she can tell when the writer is having fun. Twain had fun writing *Huck Finn*, she says. Mark Harris had fun writing the Henry Wiggen novels. Higgins had fun writing *Eddie Coyle*. Tom Wolfe always has fun.

The common denominator here is some humor and a large dose of idiosyncrasy, either in the writing or the characters or both. What's fun to write is fun to read. The dialogue in *The Friends of Eddie Coyle*—blunt, profane, spiced with wit and sarcasm—is immensely entertaining. Who doesn't savor the self-serving and mendacious bombast of those two scamps, the King and the Duke, in *Huckleberry Finn*? Who isn't eager to hear what Atticus Finch will say next, and how he will say it?

All good dialogue affords pleasure, if not fun. McCarthy's dialogue is engrossing in the way that Hemingway's is: there's pleasure in its succinctness and clarity, in the vigor of the language itself. It's *alive*. Didion's is equally spare and clean, and nobody is better at saying what *ought* to have been said than her jaded and intelligent heroines, masters of the mordant, dead-on observation or rejoinder. Lee Smith loves country music, and to read her dialogue is to hear the sweet ache of a country song.

• • •

The scraps of dialogue that follow are favorites of mine. Some are funny, some are sweet, some tense, and one is famously moralistic.

All of them give satisfaction—what *ought* to have been said. They're fun to read and could only have been fun to write.

Treasure Island's old pirate, Billy Bones, is a nightly nuisance in the Admiral Benbow Inn until Dr. Livesey has a word with him:

> The captain flapped his hand upon the table before him in a way we all knew to mean silence. The voices stopped at once, all but Dr. Livesey's; he went on as before, speaking clear and kind and drawing briskly at his pipe between every word or two. The captain glared at him for a while, flapped his hand again, glared still harder, and at last broke out with a villainous, low oath, "Silence, there, between decks!"
>
> "Were you addressing me, sir?" says the doctor; and when the ruffian had told him, with another oath, that this was so, "I have only one thing to say to you, sir," replies the doctor, "that if you keep on drinking rum, the world will soon be quit of a very dirty scoundrel!"

That exchange has stayed with me from childhood, and so has Jim's line, called across the water from the raft as Huck paddles away to reconnoiter a town:

> "Dah he goes, de old true Huck; de on'y white genlman dat ever kep' his promise to ole Jim."

Lonesome Dove is a sprawling epic rife with the violence of the old West, but in its quiet moments Larry McMurtry was able to have fun with his dialogue. Early in the novel Augustus McCrae has erected a sign at the entrance to the ranch in Lonesome Dove; the sign, like Augustus, is wordy. He has appended, UVA UVAM VIVENDO VARIA FIT:

> "What's it say, that Latin?" Call asked.

"It's a motto," Augustus said. "It just says itself." He was determined to conceal for as long as possible the fact that he didn't know what the motto meant . . .

Call was quick to see the point. "You don't know yourself," he said. "It could say anything. For all you know it invites people to rob us."

Augustus got a laugh out of that. "The first bandit that comes along that can read Latin is welcome to rob us, as far I'm concerned," he said. "I'd risk a few nags for the opportunity of shooting an educated man for a change."

This one needs no commentary:

Atticus said to Jem one day, "I'd rather you shot at tin cans in the back yard, but I know you'll go after birds. Shoot all the bluejays you want, if you can hit 'em, but remember it's a sin to kill a mockingbird."

That was the only time I ever heard Atticus say it was a sin to do something, and I asked Miss Maudie about it.

"Your father's right," she said. "Mockingbirds don't do one thing but make music for us to enjoy. They don't eat up people's gardens, they don't nest n corncribs, they don't do one thing but sing their hearts out for us. That's why it's a sin to kill a mockingbird."

Upland Game, by Howard Frank Mosher, is a favorite short story of mine. A leathery, tubercular sharpshooter and salesman of shotguns and shells has come to the tiny town of Kingdom Common in the Northeast Kingdom of Vermont. The narrator is an adolescent boy who is exceedingly proud of his big brother, Charlie. Charlie has made a bet with the sharpshooter that he can outshoot him in the woods:

"The springs in your rig are all shot to hell and gone," I said.

"No call for barbershop talk," he said, yanking at the heel of a rubber. "You was my kid, you'd be cutting a switch about now."

"You ever have any kids?"

"No, praise be."

He stood up and struggled into his overcoat and buttoned it up to the throat. In the overcoat and rubbers he . . . looked like a tramp just in off the B & M tracks.

My brother stared at him. "Aren't you going to be hot?"

"I hope so," the shooter said. "But I doubt it."

He loaded the shotgun and turned it upside down and shut one eye and squinted down the barrel.

"How is it," he said into the gun barrel, "that you ain't off in college? A smart young fella like you."

"I might go next year," Charlie said.

"He knows more than most of the professors do already," I said.

The shooter straightened up and gave a sardonic cough.

"Go ahead," I said. "Ask him a question. Any question at all."

"I just did."

One more, from *Ironweed,* an exchange at once comic and touched with sorrow:

"Whatayou been up to?" Rudy asked. "You know somebody buried up there?"

"A little kid I used to know."

"A kid? What'd he do, die young?"

"Pretty young."

"What happened to him?"

"He fell."

"He fell where?"

"He fell on the floor."

"Hell, I fall on the floor about twice a day and I ain't dead."

"That's what you think," Francis said.

You can write good dialogue. Take your time. Concentrate. Ask yourself: Where's the surprise in this speech? Where's the tension? Make every word work for you. "All his life Hemingway labored after that 'true sentence,'" wrote Alfred Kazin. You may not turn your life over to the labor, but let Hemingway's devotion to his craft, a sentence at a time, instruct you. Make it your mantra while you're writing dialogue.

LIST OF WORKS CITED:

Novels:

Conrad, Joseph: *Heart of Darkness, Lord Jim, Youth, Chance*
Dexter, Pete: *Paris Trout*
Dickens, Charles: *Bleak House, A Christmas Carol*
Didion, Joan: *Play It As It Lays, Democracy*
Faulkner, William: *The Sound and the Fury, Absalom, Absalom!,*
     Light in August, The Bear
Fitzgerald, F. Scott: *The Great Gatsby*
Gaines, Ernest J., *A Lesson Before Dying*
Harris, Mark: *Bang the Drum Slowly, The Southpaw*
Haruf, Kent: *The Tie That Binds, Plainsong*
Higgins, George V.: *The Friends of Eddie Coyle*
Hough, John: *The Last Summer, Seen the Glory, Little Bighorn*
Kennedy, William: *Ironweed, The Flaming Corsage*
Lee, Harper: *To Kill a Mockingbird*
Leonard, Elmore: *Tishomingo Blues*
McCarthy, Cormac: *All the Pretty Horses, The Crossing, Cities of the*
     Plain, No Country For Old Men, The Orchard Keeper
McMurtry, Larry: *Lonesome Dove*
Melville, Herman: *Moby Dick*

Morrison, Toni: *Beloved, Song of Solomon*
Mosher, Howard Frank: *Waiting for Teddy Williams*
Pearson, T. R.: *A Short History of a Small Place*
Sayles, John: *Union Dues*
Schulberg, Budd: *Waterfront*
Smith, Lee: *Oral History, The Devil's Dream, Fair and Tender Ladies,*
    On Agate Hill, Family Linen
Stevenson, Robert Louis: *Treasure Island*
Styron, William: *The Confessions of Nat Turner*
Twain, Mark: *Huckleberry Finn*
Tyler, Anne: *Back When We Were Grownups*
Warren, Robert Penn: *All The King's Men*
Wolfe, Tom: *A Man in Full*

Short Stories:

Ball, Bo: "It's Just One Elvis"
Carver, Raymond: "A Small Good Thing"
Faulkner, William: "Wash"
Hemingway, Ernest: "The Killers," "Fifty Grand," "The Short Happy
    Life of Francis Macomber"
Leonard, Elmore: "When the Women Come Out to Dance,"
    "Chickasaw Charley Hoke"
McPherson, James Alan: "The Silver Bullet"
Mosher, Howard Frank: "Upland Game"
Parker, Dorothy: "Arrangement in Black and White"
Proulx, Annie: "People in Hell Just Want a Drink of Water," "Pair
    a Spurs"
Runyon, Damon: "Breach of Promise"
Sayles, John: "Hoop"
Welty, Eudora: "Powerhouse"

INDEX

Smith, Lee, 8, 9, 19, 31, 55, 69, 91, 103, 122, 132
Smith, Maggie, 36–38
"Smoking Gun Tape", 14
Song of Solomon (Morrison), 1, 17, 20, 21, 120
Sound and the Fury, The (Faulkner), xi, 50, 51, 100, 101, 107
Southpaw, The (Harris), 87
Stanton, Anne, 74, 75
Stark, Willie, 70, 71, 74, 75, 80
Steiger, Rod, 61
Steinbeck, John, xii
Streep, Meryl, 62
Styron, William, 64, 125, 126
Sun Also Rises, The (Hemingway), xi
Suspense in monologues, 46–48
Sutpen, Henry, 90
Sutpen, Thomas, 102
Swerling, Jo, 88, 89

T
Talking verbs, 4–6
"Ten Rules of Writing", 4
Tension, 35–48
  definitions of, 35
  high, 43–46
Tics, avoiding, 21–23
Tie That Binds, The (Haruf), 10, 41
Tishomingo Blues (Leonard), 46
To Kill a Mockingbird (Lee), 47, 58–60
Treasure Island (Stevenson), viii, 133
Trotwood, Betsey, viii
Turner, Nat, 64, 125
Twain, Mark, 4, 57, 58, 87, 114, 115, 116, 125, 126, 132
Tyler, Anne, 8, 9, 31, 72, 74, 75, 105

U
Union Dues (Sayles), 91, 106, 108, 109
"Upland Game" (Mosher), 134

V
Verbs
  adverbs, 6
  talking, 4–6
Vernacular, using, 112–124
Victor, Harry, 79
Victor, Inez, 78, 79
Voice-activated tape recorders, 13
Voice, as physical description, 50–54

W
Waiting for Teddy Williams (Mosher), 78
Warren, Robert Penn, xii, 70, 71, 74, 75, 80
"Wash" (Faulkner), 102
Watergate tapes, 13–16, 18
Welty, Eudora, 5, 8, 9, 31, 66
"When the Women Come Out to Dance" (Leonard), 73
Where You Once Belonged (Haruf), 10
Wiggen, Henry, 85–89, 132
Wiggins, Grant, 45, 46
Wild Ones, The, 60
Wilks, Mary Jane, 87, 125
Williams, Walter, xi
Wilson, Myrtle, ix
Winslow, Allen, 38
Wolfe, Tom, 7, 8, 10, 132
Writer as hoarder, 30–33
Wyeth, Maria, 25, 29, 53

Y
Younger, Granny, 103, 104
Youth (Conrad), 84

Books from Allworth Press

Allworth Press is an imprint of Skyhorse Publishing, Inc. Selected titles are listed below.

Branding for Bloggers
by Zach Heller (5 ½ x 8 ½, 112 pages, paperback, $16.95)

Starting Your Career as a Freelance Writer, Second Edition
by Moira Anderson Allen (6 x 9, 304 pages, paperback, $24.95)

Starting Your Career as a Freelance Web Designer
by Neil Tortorella (6 x 9, 256 pages, paperback, $19.95)

Starting Your Career as a Freelance Editor: A Guide to Working with Authors, Books, Newsletters, Magazines, Websites, and More
by Mary Embree (6 x 9, 240 pages, paperback, $19.95)

Starting Your Career as a Social Media Manager
by Mark Story (6 x 9, 264, paperback, $19.95)

Publish Your Book: Proven Strategies and Resources for the Enterprising Author
by Patricia Fry (6 x 9, 264, paperback, $19.95)

The Pocket Small Business Owner's Guide to Starting Your Business on a Shoestring
by Carol Tice (5 ¼ x 8 ¼ , 224 pages, paperback, $14.95)

The Writer's Legal Guide
by Kay Murray and Tad Crawford (6x 9, 352 pages, paperback, $19.95)

The Pocket Legal Companion to Copyright: A User-Friendly Handbook for Protecting and Profiting from Copyrights
by Lee Wilson (5 x 7 ½, 320 pages, paperback, $16.95)

The Business of Writing: Professional Advice on Proposals, Publishers, Contracts, and More for the Aspiring Writer
Edited by Jennifer Lyons; foreword by Oscar Hijuelos (6 x 9, 304 pages, paperback, $19.95)

To see our complete catalog or to order online, please visit *www.allworth.com*.